FLIGHT INTO THE UNKNOWN

GISELLE ROEDER

DREAMING OF LIFE
AND LOVE IN CANADA

Book 2 of "The Nine Lives of Gila" series

Published by
Roeder Publishing
Nanaimo, B.C., Canada

Copyright © 2020 Giselle Roeder
First Edition

All rights reserved.
This book is based entirely on the memories of the author with the exception of some of the political history. No part of this publication may be reproduced in any form, or by any means, electronic or mechanical, including photocopying, recording, or any information browsing, storage, or retrieval system, without permission in writing from the author.

ISBN:
978-0-9949977-5-3

OTHER BOOKS BY GISELLE ROEDER

"Healing with Water: Kneipp Hydro-Therapy at Home" – 2000
"Sauna: The Hottest Way to Good Health" – 2002
"We Don't Talk About That" (Book 1 of "The Nine Lives of Gila" series) – 2014
"Forget Me Not" – 2016
"Ein Mensch von Gestern …Heute" – 2017
"Set Sail for Life After 50" (Book 3 of "The Nine Lives of Gila" series) - planned for September 2020

DISCLAIMER

"Flight Into The Unknown" is the story of the author's life, based on personal memories, supported by a diary and hundreds of letters. The characters in this book are real, but the names are fictitious to protect their privacy.

DEDICATION

To my family, past and present.

"Keep all special thoughts and memories for lifetimes to come. Share these keepsakes with others to inspire hope and build from the past, which can bridge to the future."
- *Mattie J.T. Stepan*

CONTENTS

Acknowledgements 1
Preface and Introduction 3
1 A Quiet Sunday Morning 5
2 A Conference Call 11
3 Two Children? 13
4 Granny Barbara 19
5 Twelve Red Roses and a Ring 29
6 Wedding Bells 37
7 E-Day - Emigration Day 49
8 North Vancouver 53
9 Winnipeg - The Prairie Town 61
10 Settling into Ordinary Family Life 67
11 Rollercoaster Year - 1965 71
12 Adenauer - a Celebration of Life 85
13 Memory Overload 89
14 767 Dorchester Avenue 95
15 New Challenges 103
16 Life Turns Upside Down 111
17 Coming into my Own 119
18 Mosquitoes, Fish and a Tapeworm 127
19 Visiting All Grandparents in Germany 131
20 French Anyone? 139
21 A Bad Accident 141
22 83 Kingsway 145
23 Giselle's Professional Skin Care 153
24 New York - New York 159
25 Back Down to Earth 165
26 Prince Charming 173
27 Dark Clouds on the Horizon 179
28 When You Dream - Dream BIG 185
29 Problems and Apologies 195
30 A Bounced Cheque 203
31 Selling the Business 209
32 An Otherwordly Experience 215
33 An Affair with Omar Sharif? 219

34 First Trip Down Under	223
35 Thoughts About Moving	229
36 Vancouver - the Beautiful	235
Epilogue	237
About the Author	239

ACKNOWLEDGMENTS

I probably would not have written this book, the sequel to "We Don't Talk About That," if you, my readers, had not kept asking, "…and then what?" You wanted to know more about my life, how the far-reaching decision I made in 1963 changed it. I thank you, whoever and wherever you are, to have kept on pushing me for several years, for not giving up on me.

You, my son Eric, who lived a large part of my 'second life' alongside me, you did the first editing and filled in some blanks, some painful moments I had consciously or unconsciously blocked out, some others deleted that caused me sleepless nights. Because of you, this book is telling the way it was. Thank you!

Christa Steinfurth, my dear old Kayak partner and lifelong friend, saved letters I had written to her over 48 years. Thank you for 'donating' them back to me – they gave me a timeline and jogged my memory - the best help I could wish for in writing this book.

Lyn Alexander, I admired you for your beautiful English writing in your 'Schellenberg Series,' consisting of four books. Thank you for becoming my friend, proof-reader, editor, and for providing the 'Preface and Introduction' to this book.

Trevor and Patricia Banks, I can't thank you enough for the incredible job you did on my cover photo. Wondering if the picture was good enough, you made it happen! I love you for it!

David Cradduck, as a graphic designer, you were the one who put the finishing touches on the book cover and provided the professional look. Thank you!

Last but not least, Trevor Cradduck, thank you for keeping me going when the going was getting tough. You spent countless hours preparing my manuscripts for publishing. After this one, you will have to do the final one in my memoir trilogy.

THANK YOU, thank you to all my friends and neighbours who encouraged me and told me:

"Keep writing - I can hardly wait to read your next book …"

FLIGHT INTO THE UNKNOWN

PREFACE AND INTRODUCTION

By Lyn Alexander, Author of 'The Schellendorf Series:'
The first part of Giselle Roeder's memoir, 'We Don't Talk About That,' captivated her readers so much they 'couldn't put the book down.' Her story reads like a mystery novel or a thriller, and it left many breathless. They are now asking for more. 'We all like a happy ending,' wrote one reader. 'What happened next?'

Perhaps a brief overview is necessary for the reader who hasn't read 'We Don't Talk About That.' Almost a history rather than a memoir, the story starts after World War One. It outlines the changes in the social makeup of many European countries, focusing primarily on post-war Germany. The discharged soldiers felt mistreated by the country's collapse after the war. People suffered unemployment and staggering inflation when half a loaf of bread cost billions and two beers a mere one-hundred billion Marks. The situation led to an Austrian's rise to power, himself a former Corporal. Hitler promised work and bread for all, and he kept his promises. The ensuing years brought a tremendous upswing of life, but it also carried Germany into World War II. The next six years brought total devastation of great cities by bombing, the invasion of Germany by the Russian army, and the atrocities the Russians committed: rape and murder, and the eviction of millions of people from the eastern part of the country.

'Gila,' as she called herself, survived those terrifying days, eventually escaping from Russian-occupied East Germany to West

Germany, encountered more trials and tribulations and finally had only one wish: To get away, get out of Germany, be free.

Ann Victoria Roberts, a bestseller writer in the UK, writes of 'We Don't Talk About That' - "A social document."

"Some parts should be read with a stiff drink beside you," writes Robert Pickles, a history writer, also in the UK. "But it is… a part of history we never heard or learned of and a missing piece of the puzzle of WWII and, if it were not so harrowing, should be required reading in schools and given the same historical, literary importance as 'The Diary of Anne Frank.'

The first book of Gila's memoir, 'We Don't Talk About That' finishes with:

"I felt as if I was in a boat on a fast river. The current takes hold of me, and all I can do is try to avoid the rocks and stay afloat - but I cannot change the direction. What would happen next? I felt apprehensive but knew in my guts that I could not change what would happen next."

Come aboard and accompany the former little Gila - who has witnessed and survived unimaginable horrors, disease, starvation, homelessness, lice and bed bugs - come along on 'a roller coaster ride through several decades of her new life.'

FLIGHT INTO THE UNKNOWN

1: A QUIET SUNDAY MORNING

The Park Hotel in Bremen, West Germany, had messed up or lost my reservation. Due to an international convention, no other hotel in the city was available. I told them:

"Sorry. I have a confirmed reservation. I will sit all night in one of those comfortable chairs in your lobby until you find a solution."

Turning around, I picked up a magazine and sat down, my luggage next to me. I watched the activity at the reception desk, phoning, discussing, and finally calling for the manager.

Embarrassed but trying to help, he offered me a maid's room above their pub in a building about a hundred yards away. I had no choice. The accommodation was clean, had a single bed, a small desk with a telephone and a sink with hot and cold water. A full bathroom and a separate toilet were in the hallway. I followed the bellman, who carried my luggage. He walked me through the pub and up the stairs. The mainly male crowd whistled and yelled, "come back down and join us." I locked myself in, lay on the bed with my legs up the wall to reduce any swelling and relaxed after many hours of driving. My dinner was a green Granny Smith apple. I kept my mind occupied browsing through the magazine 'Constance' - the one I had picked up in the reception area. Since there was nothing else to do, I read it from cover to cover, even the ads. No radio, no television. No books.

"Divorced Dad with a four-year-old daughter, looking for a new Mommy to join us in Beautiful British Columbia, Vancouver, Canada. I own a car and a building lot. Reply to…"

Hmm. Canada? It felt like a message. Did I listen to my gut feeling? The warning that I could not change what would come next - if I answered it? No. Stuck and safe in this small room above the hotel pub hidden in a large park, I started to dream about Canada. What if?

In my present state of mind, 'Oh Canada' was just the right destination for me, far enough away from Germany. The last few months had been unpleasant. My attempted rape court case had been the last straw. I was fed up with my gypsy life as a representative of a company, always being on the road. I loved my job, and I didn't mind driving, but I was longing for change. Contemplating what if - and, just as an exercise, I wrote my answer to the advert. There was no stationary, except a small notepad next to the telephone. I used five pages of it. A small photo of me happened to be in my purse. In the morning, I asked the receptionist for an envelope and a stamp. I hesitated when holding it over the slot in the letterbox - then dropped it. Did I expect a reply?

No, not really. I had almost forgotten it when, four weeks later, a thick envelope with a rather lovely letter, photographs of the man and his young daughter, and several 'Beautiful British Columbia' magazines were in my letterbox. The little girl in Canada had picked my small picture out of several hundred replies and declared,

"I want her to be my new mommy."

I wasn't sure anymore. It wasn't my style to lie in bed and think. Today I needed to concentrate and THINK. I focused on my only painting, a copy of Franz Marc's 'Red Horses' in my line of vision. A song about Canada was quite popular at the beginning of the sixties. Loosely translated, the words were, 'We buy a little house in Canada, chase the plentiful wild horses, say goodbye to our friends and invite them to come and visit us in Canada.' The catchy melody kept going through my mind endlessly. I had listened to the record after I had opened the mail.

How do you answer a letter from a total stranger who is intrigued by you and, if things work out, wants to marry you? Join

FLIGHT INTO THE UNKNOWN

him in Beautiful British Columbia, in Vancouver, one of the fascinating cities in the world? Could I take the responsibility of fulfilling a little girl's wish to be her new mommy? Was I ready, or would I come to regret leaving a busy professional life with financial independence to become a housewife and mother?

I imagined myself sitting on a bench in a playground watching my new, four-year-old daughter playing in the sandbox or pushing the swing for her. Could I trust and rely on a man I did not know? How would it be to be surrounded by strangers, not to know anybody? To live in a country on the other side of the globe with a language I hadn't mastered? Customs with which I was not familiar, existing far away from parents, siblings, relatives, and friends across the oceans? Would I get homesick? What if it does not work out? I can't just pack up and go if this child needs me, loves me, and relies on me.

My contemplation was interrupted by the ringing of the telephone. The voice at the other end was slow and deliberate.

"I am Dr. Ludwig Bader. I practice law in Wiesbaden. My son wrote to you from Canada. I thought you should know he is not a 'fly-by-night' and, naturally, my wife and I want to learn a bit more about you as well."

I was quite surprised. Was this man checking up on me? Dr. Bader made it easy. We had a friendly and open conversation. I told him about my apprehension and the thoughts which had been going through my mind. He had an answer for everything, a typical lawyer. I mentioned my work schedule would take me close to Wiesbaden in a couple of weeks. He invited me to visit and encouraged me to write the answering letter. His son, also named Ludwig, but called Louis in Canada, and little Isabelle were anxiously waiting. Dr. Bader gave me his phone number and promised to be available any time to answer questions or to have a chat. I told him my parents lived in East Germany, and except for my sister in Hamburg, I was pretty much on my own.

"A good reason to give my son a chance! Heaven knows you may like having an instant family," was Dr. Bader's last comment.

It was the middle of March 1963. An active correspondence with Louis started. The mail took a week to get from Canada to Germany and vice versa. After the first few letters, neither of us waited for any to arrive. We started to write almost daily.

Questions asked in a note on the way, were often already answered. It was as if each of us was reading the other's mind. It seemed so much easier to be open in letters than talking to a live person. Maybe it was an excellent way to get to know more about each other in a short time.

I called Dr. Bader. "Is it alright to visit you next Sunday? I am in Mannheim…"

The Bader family was very welcoming but warned me:

"Because of the soccer game, the Autobahns will be packed. If you leave early enough, you could arrive around eleven and be on time for dinner at noon. Drive carefully; we look forward to meeting you."

I was excited about this meeting. I bought a beautiful bouquet as was customary to hand to the hostess, especially on a first visit.

Parked in front of their house in a groomed neighbourhood of Wiesbaden was a black Mercedes Benz. Thinking of the son in Canada, I thought, "I hope the apple did not fall far from the tree." I felt at ease when Dr. Bader shook my hand; it was as if I knew him already. While taking the wrapping paper off the flowers before giving them to his wife, I unwittingly committed my first faux pas. My mistake was to address her as Frau Bader. Aware of facial expressions and body language, I noticed a change in her demeanour, but could not immediately figure out what I had done wrong. Later that day, when conversations flowed smoothly, she condescendingly told me I should have called her Frau Doctor.

"But you are not a doctor," I countered, committing my second faux pas.

She tried to teach me manners while I felt like a second-class citizen again, put into the role of the 'Ossie' (Easty, a person from East Germany). I had tried hard to overcome the feelings of inferiority and not be offended every time they surfaced. It was a sore spot in my emotions. I was aware of her intention to show me I was not part of their upper class, not so much through words but behaviour.

The day went well enough. There was an instant connection with Dr. Bader. He made me laugh, and we both liked finding out our birthdays were just days apart. Both of us were born under the sign Aquarius. Since Aquarius is an air sign, he called both of us 'airheads.' He talked about experiences in his profession and

FLIGHT INTO THE UNKNOWN

mentioned he had never lost a case. On one occasion, he had heard his adversary say, "Dr. Bader is asleep," to which the judge replied, "Dr. Bader is never more dangerous than when he pretends to be asleep." As the evening approached and I prepared to leave, he switched the radio on. The Autobahn to Mannheim had endless traffic jams. He decided:

"You stay here. It is not safe for you to drive. You can leave early tomorrow morning and still be on time for work."

"But, Dr. Bader, I don't even have my toothbrush…" I tried to reason with him.

"That doesn't matter; you can use a finger."

The suggestion caused a good laugh. Dr. Bader had made a decision, and he left me no choice.

A large guest room was on the lower level of the house. A thick curtain divided it into a sitting area and a bedroom with two beds. Their young son, Dietmar, who had been out with his Scout Group, had a room downstairs as well. He came to chat with me until his mother turned up, admonishing him to go to bed. I wondered how the son Louis in Canada could be thirty-six and Dietmar only eleven years old.

"Frau Doctor, you don't seem old enough to have a thirty-six-year-old son."

My comment brought a blush to her cheeks. She explained she was a second and younger wife. They had tried for twenty years to have a child and then just gave up. When she started to gain weight in her forties, she went to a health resort to lose it and was amazed when the doctor there told her,

"Nothing is wrong with your weight. You are pregnant."

Indeed, it was an exciting thought to perhaps belong to this lovely family. I spent the next weekend with them. Frau Doctor now graciously allowed me to call her Frau Bader. My mind was reeling with thoughts of everything that happened during these days.

Dr. Bader cooked the Sunday meal, and I helped him in the small kitchen. Frau Bader, elegantly dressed, set the table in the corner of the living room. Later, she and I did the dishes. Frau Bader talked about her aristocratic grandparents and of her volunteering to be a nurse during the war and meeting Dr. Bader, who had been a high-ranking officer in the German navy. She briefly mentioned his first wife, who was in an old age care home.

"We have a friendly relationship because of the three grown children, of which Louis in Canada is the youngest. He has two sisters, Barbara and Marion, both living in the United States. There was an older brother, Richard. Sadly, he did not survive his first mission at nineteen in a U-boat. He left a farewell letter for his mother. He told her he had a premonition he would not come back."

Since it was a sunny spring day, we spent the afternoon sitting around a large table on the patio, looking at photo albums. I liked Dietmar, and we made fast friends. He was keen to show me childhood pictures of his half-siblings as well as many of himself. His mother mentioned they recently talked about *the birds and the bees.* Dietmar had listened attentively and then stated,

"So Dad did it four times with his first wife and only once with you."

2: A CONFERENCE CALL

Coming home from Wiesbaden, I found a letter from my parents. Mail from East to West Germany took longer than a letter from Canada. My father had written. He was very concerned about my newest adventure; going to Canada to marry a stranger, a divorced man with a child was unthinkable.

"Are you out of your mind? Aren't you old enough to think this through? How do you know this is all honest and above board? You can't just judge this man by his handwriting, his nice way of writing and the beautiful pictures he sends you. For all you know, he might be a talented con-man. Gila, I am worried and quite anxious about you."

I started to answer his letter and tell him about my meeting with the Canadian man's parents in Wiesbaden when my phone rang.

A male voice I did not know was asking for a person who wasn't me. The voice explained something about a conference call regarding a business deal. I made a joke and suggested maybe I should be involved. Then another male voice cut in and the third one. They were all from different cities. It was fun to quip with no one knowing who I was. Finally, they decided they must have dialed the wrong number. They asked for mine, but I did not reveal it.

"Too bad," the first voice said, "I would love to talk to you again. You are fun! I'll try all kinds of combinations of the number to get you again."

He had an incredible laugh, a throaty laugh such as I had never heard before. It was contagious, and it put a smile on my face. A day later, he phoned me again.

"Oh! Hi, there you are. I had just switched the last two digits," he laughed, "it wasn't difficult at all to find you again. Do you mind us having a chat?"

A few weeks hence, I met Hannes, the wrong-number man. For years I had never met anybody I liked well enough. Now I felt obligated to the Bader family and guilty liking Hannes. What was I to do? I knew what my dad would say. Why did fate give me a choice at this time? Hold on to my dream of going to Canada and be part of a family or stay in familiar surroundings? Would Mr. E. from my past turn up again and ruin it for me? He had promised to break up any relationship I would ever have. Or shoot me and then himself.

"If I can't have you, then nobody will." Those had been his parting words. He had been stalking me for years, always knew where I was, sent flowers, and I suspected he might have an agency watching me.

After a few more meetings in Hanover and one in Hamburg, Hannes made quite clear he was serious about me. Naturally, I had told him about my pen pal in Canada. I couldn't stop talking about it. Little Isabelle's photo was in my purse or on my night table in my hotel. I was in love with her. She was always on my mind. Her picture was the last I looked at in the evening and the first in the morning.

I felt carefree and happy when meeting Hannes but remained elusive, afraid I would get hurt, or I would hurt him. I was always honest. I thought it was one way to keep him from having ideas that I could not accept. He was separated; his divorce not yet finalized. They had no children, and his wife wanted to be free again. Hannes always planned fun things, like spending a day at the great Zoo in Hamburg or visiting the beautiful Herrenhäuser Gardens in Hanover, where we saw 'A Midsummer Night's Dream' by Shakespeare on the outdoor theatre stage. I remember the dark velvety sky with millions of twinkling stars. Sitting next to Hannes, I wished for one to fall, a chance to make a wish, thinking of little Isabelle. No shooting star appeared that night, they were all far away and seemed to be mocking me.

3: TWO CHILDREN?

By the end of June 1963, I had visited the Bader family quite a few times; they behaved as if everything was already decided. I often wondered if all the attention was only to secure a suitable wife for their son and a new mother for the granddaughter? I felt overwhelmed but also enjoyed the sense of belonging and was proud to be accepted into this classy family.

Dr. Bader had two brothers. All three men had been high-ranking officers during WWII: Dr. Bader in the navy, another brother in the army and the third in the high command of the air force. The last had been tried and exonerated during the Nuremberg trials. Frau Bader often mentioned her aristocratic grandmother. I checked the 'Who's Who book' and never did find the name. I wished to come up with something special about my own family. I checked with Aunt Irene, my dad's sister, who had always been very much involved with our ancestry. She and my parents lived in the same village. Her answering letter and the story she related delighted me. I loved it:

"Once upon a time and only a few generations back, there was a shepherd in our family of tradesmen. He worked for a large Pomeranian Estate. He was quite handsome, and the daughter of the owner fell in love with him. They were not allowed to marry. She chose to live with him, and her family disowned her. She became pregnant and bore a son. They christened him Christian Sydow. Her parents had made sure the girl dropped the 'von' from her name, which would have identified her association with her aristocratic family von Sydow. She lived a commoner's life with her beloved shepherd and their son Christian."

Christian Sydow appears in my family's genealogy. Does the small city of Sydowsaue, where my granny's brother lived before the eviction by the Polish army in 1945, have some relevance to the name Sydow? Aue stands for meadow. Sydowsaue in English would be Sydow's Meadow. I was happy to have found a romantic, aristocratic ancestor, even if he was born out of wedlock. Could I impress Frau Bader? I was impressed by what this girl had done. I would also leave my family if I loved a man that much and would move to the end of the world to be with him.

One day, out of the blue, Dr. Bader stood in front of me and put a thin gold chain with a globe pendant of planet Earth around my neck. He looked at me, and then turned it to the continent of North America, pointed to the West Coast of Canada and said:

"Look, here you will live. There is Vancouver, where Louis and Isabelle are waiting for you."

I was speechless. I did not know what to say or do, so I took the little golden globe in my hand, looked at it and whispered,

"Thank you."

My blood pressure must have dropped because I felt dizzy and had to sit down. When I wrote to my dad about this episode, he wrote back,

"Sure, now they've put you on a chain. Gila, Gila, what did you get yourself into this time?" He could not wrap his head around my apparent decision to emigrate to Canada.

The next letter from Louis gave me the answer to my questions regarding Isabelle. Why did she live with her father and not with her mother? Louis revealed Isabelle had a younger sister living in Germany with an aunt of her biological mother. He wrote of his separation and divorce settlement and the reason why he was the guardian of Isabelle while his ex-wife was the guardian of Doris. The children's mother had only agreed to it because her Aunt Anna promised to take care of Doris, who was nine months old. He and his wife had separated earlier, and when they had reconciled for the sake of Isabelle, Doris had been the result. Aunt Anna was visiting them in Canada, taking care of the household and the children while both parents worked. Isabelle was two at the time.

FLIGHT INTO THE UNKNOWN

The reason for the divorce had been another man. Louis mentioned that all his friends knew of his former wife's affair; he had been the last because nobody wanted to tell him. His father had advised him to hire a detective who was able to take incriminating photos.

Adultery was one of the only reasons for a court to grant a divorce at that time. During the Court proceedings, the children's mother stated she wanted nothing to do with raising her children. If she were obliged to care for them, she would go to a doctor and have herself declared a mentally unfit mother. His ex-wife had told Louis that her Italian boyfriend did not want a woman with children. After the divorce, Aunt Anna took baby Doris with her to Germany. Once Kirsten was free, her boyfriend did not want her at all, because he was Catholic and could not marry a divorcee or a woman of a different faith.

What a sad story. I was distraught. How, or why, would any mother not want her children? Not fight for them? I could not understand it. Must one be crazy in love to do such a thing? I talked to my sister Christel in Hamburg, who was married and had a little girl. Her sunshine Delia was my goddaughter. I kept this news from my parents. They would be even more against me taking the dangerous step of joining a stranger in Canada.

I was deeply attached to little Isabelle. I could not give up the dream of being her new mommy. I talked to Hannes about it, trying to analyze my situation. He had become a terrific friend. Hannes understood my dilemma, tried to reason with me. He knew how involved I had become with the Bader family and how I did not know how to disentangle myself. I liked Dr. Bader, didn't want to disappoint him and have him say, "a typical Ossie, unreliable."

I was embarrassed to admit to Louis how I felt about his revelations and that I was not ready to trust my life to him. Sure, his divorce verdict was 'not guilty' according to the law at the time - but then, it always takes two to tango. I tried to put myself in Kirsten's shoes. If you are unhappy with your life, and you meet someone who makes you happy, despite having two small children? What if you believe your lover is what he appeared to be? I could not fathom leaving my two babies. How could she? Even knowing her aunt and the father would do their best for them?

I needed to speak to Dr. Bader. By this time, he had insisted I call him Vati (Father) and Frau Bader allowed me to call her Mui. Vati helped me see the other side of the coin using his lawyer's voice. He told me how much he and his wife had been against Louis' marriage. Louis had been in the hospital for a stomach operation in Cologne, and Kirsten was the nurse who looked after him. She was flirtatious and had seduced him. Louis was a virgin and became taken with her. Family arguments only strengthened his feelings in wanting to marry her, and he did. They talked of emigrating to Canada, and he applied for permission at the Consulate. They both hoped to have a fresh start without family interference. He left Germany about a year before his new bride could follow him. He found a job, saved money for her fare and found a place for them to live.

"I had someone keep an eye on her," Vati confided, "after Louis left for Canada, she had an affair in Cologne, but Louis would not believe us."

He mentioned that he had never helped Louis with the wedding or money for the emigration, but he had happily paid for all the associated costs of the divorce. He also sent a monthly sum to Aunt Anna for Doris' maintenance since Louis could not afford to send money. I admitted I would not have entered into a pen-pal relationship had I known there were two children involved. I was working in the alternative health field and had no experience with raising small children despite having helped to raise my three younger sisters when I was a child myself. I cried and told Vati,

"I don't feel strong enough to handle it."

He took me in his arms, patted my back and stated as a matter of fact:

"You'll never have Doris. She'll be enrolled in a prestigious boarding school in the Rhineland when she is of age. I'll make sure she always has everything she ever needs."

Yes, I thought bitterly, she'll have everything she'll ever need, but no parents. The episode left me in a subdued mood for days, and I was glad to be busy. A dark cloud had hidden the bright sunny sky over Vancouver as I knew it from the photos and had imagined it to be. How could I get out of this without disappointing all these people and thinking wrong thoughts of me?

FLIGHT INTO THE UNKNOWN

More letters from Louis arrived, and his plans for the future lightened my load somewhat. He knew of my aversion to smoking. I had confessed I would never marry a smoker. He commented,

"Oh, that's no problem. I was at a party last night, and when I got in my car, I just sat there, had a cigarette and realized I was not enjoying it at all. The fresh night air was so much better. I just threw it and my remaining cigarettes out of the window, followed by the lighter. I have not smoked since."

In another letter, he wrote, "I had a dream. We were at the beach, and you were running ahead of me in the nude. I tried to catch you but I couldn't. You were faster."

I took this dream for what it was, just a dream, but it disturbed me. Silly, maybe. I felt Louis had no right to dream of me in the nude. Now, many years later and wiser and, having delved into psychology and dream analysis, I see it differently. His dream was a warning for me; I could or should have followed it.

FLIGHT INTO THE UNKNOWN

4: GRANNY BARBARA

One of the next letters from Louis contained an invitation to visit his biological mother in her care home. He had not seen her in many years. I was curious about her, wanted to know more about her, hear her side of the divorce and her relationship with her former husband, Dr. Bader and his new wife.

    I met a lovely lady, entirely different from Vati's second wife. She seemed a little distant but entirely welcoming. In her room, full bookcases covered almost a whole wall; next to a recliner close to the only window were more books stacked up, and even more on the table. The room looked messy but in a comfortable way. Photographs of her four children, many of little Isabelle and a few taken when Doris was a tiny baby, graced every other available spot on shelves, side tables, and the windowsill. Her dress was old-fashioned and not of high quality. Her face had a thousand wrinkles, and her eyes occasionally took on a conspiring look when she told me of her youngest son: Louis in Canada.

    Having three children, she had not wanted another and had tried to end the pregnancy. She smiled as she talked of things she did: jumping from a table, taking scalding baths, and drinking strong digestive tea.

    "Oh, this baby was stubborn and wanted to be born, nothing produced the result I wanted. Poor little guy, he had to fight for his life right from the beginning. He deserves love; he grew up to be a nice reliable man. I love him dearly and am glad things worked out the way they did. My eldest son Richard was the apple of my eye, and little Louis soon figured that out. My father enrolled them both in the same boarding school. Louis was only seven years old when he had to go far away from Berlin. That was years before the war."

She took a deep breath and seemed to contemplate what to tell me next.

"In those days, my husband was away most of the time. I suspected an affair but then found out that aside from working at his low-paying government job, he secretly had been studying law. One day he came home and proudly told me that I was now married to Doctor Ludwig Bader. He finally impressed my father, who had supported us financially for many years. Father had been against our relationship. I was two years older than Ludwig; it was not the norm in our circles. He believed Ludwig was after me only because I came from an established, wealthy aristocratic family. I am not sure how to phrase it, but in my way, I loved this young man. Maybe it was a bit of a rebellion; I wanted it my way, and I got it my way."

Laughing, she added, "I think I was afraid I wouldn't find another husband because I was already in my mid-twenties and getting old. All my younger friends were already married, and some even had children."

I did not dare to show curiosity or ask questions. A knock on the door revealed it was time for tea.

"Mother Superior, come in! Thanks for the tea. Please, meet my future daughter-in-law, Gisela, she is going to be my granddaughter Isabelle's new mommy and my son is thrilled they have found each other."

I got up to shake Mother Superior's hand. Mother Superior stayed for tea and asked me many questions. I felt the blood rising to my face and sank back down into my chair, utterly helpless. I felt overwhelmed by Granny Barbara's statements, and Mother Superior began to quiz me regarding my own and my family's history. Nobody like her had ever quizzed me. I did not know how to sidestep her questions. I knew the Baders were not Catholic, and I was not either. If my mother had obeyed her father, I would be half Jewish, or my family would most likely not even be alive. I thought it unusual for the elder Mrs. Bader to be in a Catholic home. Maybe she could not afford anything else? Granny Barbara urged me to come back soon when I finally was able to say goodbye. There was so much more she wanted to tell me.

I revisited her two weeks later. A young nun was delivering the tea; we had the afternoon to ourselves. My visits seemed therapeutic for the old lady. She had no other visitors.

"Oh, Gisela," she hugged me tightly; "you are a Godsend for me. I didn't want to live anymore. I feel lonely with only the characters in books for my company. My daughters live in America. They have no children, and I lost hope of them having any. Louis and Isabelle live in Canada. None of them seem to have the means to fly home to visit me. I cannot afford to send them money for a flight. Isabelle's younger sister Doris is being cared for by Aunt Anna and her mother's parents. She lives close to Frankfurt, but I have no access. I don't even know her."

She choked up, and her old eyes misted over. A few tears found their way down her wrinkled, colourless face. She tried hard to overcome her emotions. She patted a chair, urged me to sit down close to her, lit a cigarette and puffed a few perfect smoke rings into the air above her. It was the one thing I didn't like about her, her constant smoking. Several ashtrays were around her room, all filled with cigarette stubs. How often might they be emptied? I wondered, but I didn't ask.

After she had sufficiently recovered, she shared memories of her own family.

"My family lived in a beautiful villa in the prestigious Grunewald, a park-like area of Berlin. My father was an avid collector of First Edition books, especially Theodor Fontane. It was his most famous collection. Adolf Hitler and even international collectors wanted to buy it, but Dad had declared that he would never sell it. When the bombings of Berlin started, Hitler insisted on placing the Theodor Fontane collection in a special bunker that contained art and lots of confiscated items from Jewish families. My father, Richard von Kehler, had no choice but to agree. The bombings eventually destroyed Hitler's art bunker, but my parent's villa had survived. Here, the books would have survived too. They had been worth millions."

Theodore Fontane was considered the most distinguished German writer of the 19th century. His last publications were 'The Stechlin' and 'Effie Briest.' Granny gave me 'Effie Briest' to read.

The tale of adultery set in the Bismarck time of Germany shattered me. I compared it to 'Anna Karenina' by Tolstoy, which, I admit, had the same effect on me. Thomas Mann, a renowned author, commented in 1919 that 'Effie Briest' is one of the most important books ever written. An English translation is available, and a movie was successful during those years.

In 1936 Richard von Kehler published a book: 'Eighty-nine previously unpublished Letters and handwritten Notes by Theodore Fontane' with his comments.

"Gisela, books were only one hobby of my father. He was an airship pioneer and heavily involved in the development of this industry. He supervised the launch and landings of the early trials in Bitterfeld. He was heavily involved in building the first Zeppelin, 'Graf Zeppelin,' which circumnavigated the world without mishap and also the 'Hindenburg,' which exploded and burned while attempting to land in Manchester/New York in May 1937. Bismarck, the chancellor of Germany, was his close friend. Wait, let me show you some pictures..."

Richard von Kehler was also the President of the German Aero Club. He wrote a song about his feelings when flying in an airship, and his nephew Hans von Kehler set it to music. Granny showed me all the documents. I felt dizzy learning about such a distinguished ancestry.

Granny went on to tell me how her father was instrumental in the development of the airline industry right from the beginning. He established the Wright Brother's Flugmaschinen (Flight Machines) company in Germany. When she mentioned her father's company in Stralsund, I told her about my life in that city. I reminisced about a villa I had visited for a dance in 1954 and the weird premonitions I had encountered as I wandered through its rooms. It was as if I knew the place. I told her about the incredible Persian rug in one room, and how I had stood there, rooted to the spot. I had never seen one so large and so beautiful. The villa was located almost across from the City Theatre and next to the statue of Ferdinand von Schill. The large backyard served as an open-air restaurant during the summer, overlooking the Baltic Sea. There were three more large villas between this and our boathouse, where I was a member of the competitive kayak club. Granny almost jumped out of her chair.

FLIGHT INTO THE UNKNOWN

"Oh my God, that was our house! Gisela, tell me more. What became of it, how come you went dancing there?"

She was quiet when she heard it was the Gewerkschafts-Haus, the Union Clubhouse and belonged to everyone in the Communist East German Republic. Every working man or woman was a member of the Union and fees were automatically deducted from salaries. She sank deeper into her chair when she heard of the large photo of Stalin and the red Soviet flag on the dark wood-panelled wall in what was the executive boardroom with a polished table surrounded by twenty-four chairs on that beautiful rug.

"Yes, I remember," she whispered, "that was our dining room. At Christmas and New Year, we rolled up the rug for dancing. Once, our maid brought in the turkey for my father to carve. She slipped, and the bird slid across the floor. My mother, seated straight as a queen at one end of the table, said, "Emma, pick it up and bring in the other one." Naturally, there was no other one, but everybody around the table smiled and might have believed it. Dear God, girl, you bring back so many memories of my younger years..."

She wanted to know everything about my life and especially my experiences in Stralsund. I told her about my kayaking, the competitions, my evening school courses in the prestigious Hansa School and my escape to Berlin, which led to my life in Hanover. She got excited and told me about her brother, Dr. Rudolf von Kehler and his wife, Hildegard. They had two teenage daughters, Susanne and Regina. She had phoned them after meeting me the first time and had a long conversation about Louis and me. They were living in Hanover and expected me to visit the next time I was at home. Another Hanover couple, Hans von Kehler and his wife Antje, had also extended an invitation through Granny. Their daughter was a favourite cousin of Louis. They had played together when they were children and gone camping when they were teenagers. Known as Mausi, but her real name was Christine.

I looked forward to going back home to Hanover to make arrangements to meet my future relatives. Marrying my pen pal and becoming little Isabelle's new mommy, began to look more enticing and exciting.

GISELLE ROEDER

Sailing and Eating Smoked Eel

My first call went to the Dr. Rudolf von Kehler family. They invited me for a Sunday noon dinner. I was surprised they lived in rather simple circumstances in an old apartment building that had survived the bombing. It was nothing grand as their name and the background story I had heard from Granny suggested. I knew that 88% of Hanover had been destroyed by bombing during the last year of the war. The von Kehler riches had evaporated after the fall of the *Thousand-Year-Reich*. Most of their holdings and companies had been in East Germany, where the new rulers nationalized everything. People were supposed to be equal; nobody had more than their neighbour. They frowned upon aristocratic and academic titles; the labourer was king. Rudolf and Granny Barbara's father, Richard von Kehler, had died in Berlin in 1943. He, Rudolf, had been in charge of the little left of once upon a time, thousands of employees in three companies. The largest company and headquarters in Berlin did not survive the bombs; every last man lost in the army. One company in Frankfurt/Oder had supplied tires, and other rubber ware to Hitler's troops, the one in Stralsund had manufactured balloons and parachutes.

Luckily, the Kehler women and children had been evacuated to Nordeck, a small town in the west of Germany, far away from Berlin. Nordeck was the place where all their children attended the prestigious boarding school. Rudolf had escaped with his sailboat, loaded with parachute silk, to Denmark during the last days of the war. His boat sank, but he had it lifted after the war ended at the beginning of May 1945. Once the aftermath of the war had settled down, he came home with his silk and met all his relatives in Nordeck. The women started to unravel the rolls of silk, and Granny Barbara knitted sweaters to exchange on the black market for food. Her oldest daughter Marion became quite a knitter as well. By this method, they lived through the period of starvation. But just like my family, they consumed a lot of turnips: turnip soup, turnip stew, turnip bread. Talking and laughing about turnips, they couldn't believe I still liked this vegetable. Now, all there was left of the Kehler fortune was a new small sewing room in Celle. It employed a few women to make or repair garments.

FLIGHT INTO THE UNKNOWN

The proceeds hardly paid for his sister Barbara's Catholic care home.

They had a sailboat on the Steinhuder Meer, a vast artificial inland lake not far from Hanover. We went sailing on the weekend after our first meeting and had a wonderfully happy, relaxed sunny day on the boat. I felt comfortable with the family and was accepted as one of them, addressing them as Uncle Rudi and Aunt Hildegard. Susanne, the eldest daughter, had invited a boisterous boyfriend who made us all laugh so hard we almost cried. He wore an old-fashioned black and white horizontally striped bathing costume covering his body from the shoulders nearly to the ankles. Being quite a gymnast, he clowned around, jumping and diving off the boat, clambering back on and couldn't get enough of it. The girls, Susanne and Regina, joined in, but I had not brought a bathing suit. I had experienced nearly drowning a few times, and I didn't like to get my head submerged underwater. Instead, I wore Uncle Rudi's captain cap and was allowed to sail the boat. I had only navigated my little paddle boat in Stralsund with five-and-a-half square meters of sail. This sailboat was the real thing, by God, it was fun.

We stopped at the lovely village for lunch. The delicacy of Steinhude was buns with smoked eel. The eels were living in the lake. I had never eaten them before; they tasted a bit like smoked herring but much greasier. I was in paradise for the day. I could count days like this in my life on just one hand. Funny, but I didn't even once think of the Baders and their so much more formal behaviour, always making me feel like a second-class citizen. With these people, I was just me, laughing with them, joking and happy with them. They were aristocrats but never even mentioned it.

Africa

The Hans von Kehler family lived in a suburb of Hanover in a cozy house with a small garden. The reception was a bit more reserved but not unfriendly by the couple who soon became Uncle Hans and Aunt Antje. I wasn't sure if Antje was part English or had grown up in England because she talked about it a lot. Their son Wolfgang studied or lived there. She didn't smile or laugh easily but was a perfect hostess. We drank tea out of beautiful, fragile porcelain teacups; the table was covered with a lace tablecloth with hand-stitched flowers, matching the teacups design. I remember the room with the dappled sunlight cut by the drawn voile curtains. Once the talk came to Mausi, their daughter in Africa, the conversation got lively.

"Mausi! Oh, our Mausi! She is quite a character! She and Louis had a lot of fun in the Zoo Gardens in Berlin when they were not even ten. They put an empty wallet on a fishing line, placed it in the middle of a path and hid behind a bush. When someone wanted to pick it up, they pulled it away, startling the people. They repeated this until a disgruntled older man tried to catch them and warned he would pull them by their ears. God knows what else those two can tell. You'll have to ask Louis!"

Mausi was married to Dr. Rüdiger Sachs, a zoologist who worked in Africa with the famous father & son team Bernhard and Michael Grzymek. They tracked the great migrations and were instrumental in establishing protected areas and parks for the wild animals. The Grzymeks had written the book, 'Serengeti Shall Not Die,' in the late fifties; it is still available, even a movie was produced. Sadly, the younger man, Michael Grzymek, had died in a plane crash when his tiger-coloured plane collided with a large bird. His father carried on the work. I remember when the newspapers were full of news about the older man's tragic death, also in a plane crash. Cousin Mausi lived in a lovely house in Africa and Aunt Antje was smiling when she told me she was always complaining about being bored. She had become quite an accomplished tennis player since there was nothing else to do. She had four children, it should have kept her busy, but it didn't. She had told her parents,

"I am bored. You can't just sit around with other bored white ladies, play tennis or drink cocktails all day. I am not even allowed to make my bed or put my sweaty laundry in the washer. Besides nursing my babies, I am not even allowed to attend to my children. When I attempt to do something, my coloured maids and the nannies protest, afraid I'm taking their jobs away."

They had four maids in the house and a couple of male outdoor helpers for garden work and protection. It was very inexpensive to have African help. It cost only the equivalent of 50 cents per person a day, and they ought to provide as many jobs as possible. I could only wonder about such a world. I brought up the tale 'Gone with the Wind', the American War of Independence, and the freeing of slaves in America.

"You are right. But these people are not slaves and are treated very nicely. We have visited at the birth of each child. There is a lot of love and trust between my grandchildren and the servants, also with Mausi and Rüdiger. Maybe not everybody treats them like they do. There are groups in particular areas who try to change the system, and there are fights. We dare to say that 'Gone with the Wind' or something like it might happen in Africa as well. We are glad Mausi and Rüdiger still have their house in Eschwege they can come back to."

Now I knew three families related to Louis in Canada. Each one was living in a very different world.

FLIGHT INTO THE UNKNOWN

5: TWELVE RED ROSES AND A RING

The next time I visited Granny Barbara, I had to promise to marry her son Louis. A letter for me had arrived at her address. I let her read it. He had popped the question. She was incredibly happy and looked like a young girl, even with all her wrinkles.

When I dropped the bombshell about the proposal, the Baders couldn't be more delighted. Vati brought up a bottle of my favourite Rheingau wine from his cellar. I told Vati about my intention to fly to Vancouver for a short holiday to meet Louis and Isabelle before I made a final decision. He did not like my plan at all.

"It costs so much money, the two of you can put it to better use. Think about it, Gisela. You'll want to furnish an apartment the way you like it; maybe you might even plan on building a home in the not too distant future. No, my girl, you don't have to fly to Vancouver. Louis is coming at the end of September. The family they live with will look after Isabelle. Don't worry your pretty little head so much. You love me, don't you? Then trust me. You'll never get a nicer father-in-law than me."

He winked at me, and that was that. I did not want to upset the apple cart. I wrote to Louis that I'd consider marrying him if we both like each other enough when we meet in person. I told him about my thoughts.

"Maybe we are in love with love and not with each other, and it is not a strong enough base to build a life on."

I truly believed I was in love with love. I was living a dream, a romance novel, and wasn't quite sure yet of the ending.

Louis' next letter was very joyful. He was sure of our life together. He made plans for his visit in September and told me a registered letter would arrive within a few days.

"Please be at home at noon on the 17th of July. I'll call you. I look forward to a good conversation."

Both of us had been very reserved when he had phoned once before. I didn't know what to expect, but the registered letter answered all my questions. It contained a ring, a wedding ring, such as is typical for German couples. When engaged, you wear the ring on the left ring finger, at the wedding, it would be transferred over to the right hand.

He suggested we get engaged during the telephone conversation. Louis would put a ring on his left ring finger in Canada, and I was to do the same in Hanover. My goodness - he was thirty-six, and I was twenty-nine years old! How could we do this, like a couple of romantic teenagers? Well, we did.

Late in the morning on the 17th, my doorbell rang. A dozen long-stemmed red roses were delivered. I sat next to the telephone at noon, not sure at all but in some way enjoying the novelty. Louis did all the talking, and I was quiet, just listening. Isabelle's little voice came across the ocean, and I was as soft as butter when she said, 'Mommy, I love you.' After the ring ceremony, I thanked him for the beautiful roses.

"My father has sent those. He offered to do it for me."

Did he give him my ring size too? I wondered. I had a habit of taking off my onyx ring when helping in the kitchen and often left it on the window sill.

Instead of flying to Vancouver, I spent my two weeks holiday in August 1963 on the Isle of Mallorca in Spain. It was the first time I had ever left Germany, flying to a foreign country. I booked a lovely little hotel close to a secluded beach. Vati drove me to the Frankfurt Airport in his black Mercedes, and I felt like a celebrity. He told me about a car trip they took to Switzerland when Dietmar was between three and four years old.

"I had bought myself a Rolex watch in Switzerland, for my wife a beautiful bracelet, and the boy received a special wind-up toy car he wanted. We got a big smoked ham as well. On our return, we were stopped by the customs officer at the border for the usual passport control. I wore my expensive watch and leaned my arm out the car window, not hiding it at all. Asked what we were bringing back, I declared some Swiss chocolate, a big ham and the young man in the back had an expensive car he should better check out. Dietmar was afraid the officer would confiscate the car he held in his hands. But the officer checked it and gave it back to him with a smile, telling him to take good care of it. He asked me where I have hidden the ham. With a wink, I said, "I am sitting on it", after that, the officer laughed and just waved me on."

"Did you have one, a ham?" He answered my question in the affirmative. Only Dr. Bader could get away with things like that.

It was my second flight; the first had been the one from Berlin to Hanover, paid for by the Allied powers following my escape from East Germany in 1955, after three weeks of being interrogated. I had not been able to tell them what they wanted to know: How many trains crossed the bridge to the island of Rügen, and how many tanks or canons were loaded? Did I know of an underground shelter for all the war material? I did not know the answers.

The weather in Spain was fantastic. I understood why so many German and English senior citizens spent their winters in Spain. Pleasant weather and less than half the cost of living even made it attractive for a lot of wealthy people to buy second homes in Spain. I shared a bright bedroom with Marianne, a lovely lady from the University City of Göttingen, who became a good friend. It was great just doing nothing, being lazy, reading or swimming. A handsome, tall young man joined us in the water and at the beach. He was well educated and an engaging conversationalist. His movements when swimming were as elegant as a seal, but he waddled on land. He told us he had suffered polio as a child. He became interested in me. I flaunted my engagement ring and talked about my future in Canada and my little daughter. Marianne and Helmut tried hard to talk me out of it, but I had my dream, and I wanted to dream it. I was surprised when I received a postcard a month later, signed by both of them. Helmut was visiting Marianne in her hometown. Marianne and I exchanged letters for a while after my emigration, and I wonder if they might have married.

On my return, Dr. Bader, his wife, and Dietmar were waiting for me at the airport in Frankfurt. I was radiant, relaxed and tanned. They had a lot of news for me. Louis was coming to Germany on the 9th of October. They had booked our wedding for the 19th in the Marktkirche, a beautiful church in Wiesbaden.

"Louis has to fly back to Canada at the end of October. He is pleased to have a family wedding and is excited to see as many family members as possible. His sister Barbara has asked Louis to bring Isabelle and stop for a couple of days at her home in Washington, D.C. She offered to pay the airfare for Isabelle in place of a wedding present."

The noon wedding reception was to be in a small, elegant hotel in Bad Schwalbach. Mui had already talked to the chef about the menu. Later, everybody would meet again in the Bader house for a celebration and a farewell for the new couple before they left on a short honeymoon.

"We'll probably be a dozen people. Do you have anybody you'd like to invite? We assume your parents will not be able to join us, living behind the iron curtain. What about your sister from Hamburg?"

The energy I had felt earlier was gone. I was overwhelmed. I sat in the back of the car with Dietmar, holding his hand. He looked at me and promised,

"You tell Louis if he doesn't treat you right, he will have to answer to me."

I loved this eleven-year-old boy who seemed so much younger than I was at his age. During the Russian invasion, having witnessed rapes and murders, always hungry, walking for three weeks with thousands of other evicted people next to the Russian war machinery on its way to Berlin, and sleeping under the stars, I had grown up fast. Did I dream then, or was I dreaming now? Were they talking about MY wedding? Should they not have discussed this with me? I knew they meant well. I should have been grateful to belong to such a friendly family who took matters into their own hands and organized everything. But I didn't appreciate it at all; on the contrary, I had a severe case of cold feet.

"Ohhh… I have to think about it. It's all coming up too fast."

FLIGHT INTO THE UNKNOWN

...and the door slowly opened

Mui planned everything. But there was no way I would give her the satisfaction of seeing my face when I met my fiancé for the first time.

I wrote to Louis, asking him how he felt about it. He agreed with me. We needed a few minutes of privacy before we faced his father and stepmother. I wished we could keep on writing letters to each other. It was not dangerous; it was romantic; our correspondence was spontaneous and open and honest. We knew more about each other after three months than people who had dated for two years. Maybe this was the only way for me to be in love. I was dreaming and most certainly was in love with love. I was not in love with the man in Canada who sent beautiful pictures of his little daughter and wrote enthusiastic letters outlining our future life.

Louis' and little Isabelle's arrival day was close, our wedding day ten days hence. On the day of their arrival, I was lecturing at Marburg University. I could not be at the Airport in Frankfurt but would arrive at the Bader residence long after dinner. I cooked up a plan to see Louis on my own.

"Louis, there is an entrance door on the lower level of the house. Can you unlock that door quietly? I will sneak in and wait for you in the small bedroom at around nine PM. Hopefully, nobody will get suspicious and follow you downstairs."

It was dark when I arrived. I parked my car a couple of blocks away from the Bader's house. A vase with a gorgeous dark pink rose stood at the entrance door. I was shaking with anticipation. My father was right. What on earth was I thinking? Marrying a divorced man I didn't know, a man with two little daughters, not one daughter as initially disclosed? I breathed deeply and prayed to God, 'please, give me strength.' Did I make my bed and now have to sleep in it? It was my mother's philosophy. A hundred thousand thoughts went through my head while I quietly descended the stairs to the lower garden with a hopefully unlocked door to get into the house. Before I entered, I went up another stairway to look into the brightly lit living room picture window. It all seemed very cozy. The family sat around the oval table with the built-in comfortable bench and chairs and had fancy wine glasses in front of them. Dr.

Bader was a wine connoisseur, and I could just imagine how he had carefully picked a special bottle from his extensive wine cellar.

Heaven help me! I took one look at Louis, and I did not like him. Was I engaged to this man? Was this the man who wrote such beautiful letters? Was this the man with the excellent handwriting? He looked very much like his mother, even closer to her age, not nearly as good-looking as in his photographs. He looked stressed. He looked gaunt. Maybe it was the jet lag. Isabelle was not there. He had mentioned in his last letter she would probably be asleep. She would meet her new mommy the next morning. Think, Gisela, think! My instinct was to run to my car and drive away - but no, I couldn't do that. Vati, the lawyer, had told me once one could be sued for broken promises. I was afraid. I needed to go into the room downstairs, wait and see what would happen. Maybe he would not feel attracted to me either. Possibly everything would be different tomorrow. But the poor kid, she was so looking forward to having a new mommy.

I retraced my steps and went into the house quietly. I walked into the guest room I had used previously, left the door slightly open, switched on the night table lamp, pulled off my shoes and lay down on the bed. I started to shiver. A rolled-up woollen blanket was at my feet. I pulled it over me and tried hard to stifle my nervousness. It did not take long until I heard footsteps coming down the stairs, and there he was: Louis from Canada with a sheepish grin on his face. The smile helped, and I had a better feeling about him than just looking at him through the window. He pulled a stool close to the bed and held my hand. Did we talk? I don't remember. We just looked and grinned at each other. He mentioned Mui would not be happy about our plan to meet privately and that there was a rose at the entrance for me.

"I know," I whispered, "I've seen it."

Only five or six minutes later, we heard light steps coming down the stairs. They stopped in front of the now-closed door. Mrs. Bader entered by slowly opening the door wide.

"You," she accosted me in a rather loud and disappointed tone, "how could you! I put a rose for you at the main door."

With that, she bent over me, lifted the blanket and uttered,

"Oh. You are dressed. Get up. Get out of the house where you came in. Ring the bell at the main door. That's the way you do it.

FLIGHT INTO THE UNKNOWN

At least Vati will see you there. You, Louis, you bad boy, you come with me."

You did as Mrs. Bader tells you. When I rang the bell at the main door and stood there like a schoolgirl, Dr. Bader's greeting and a big hug made me feel better. Louis was standing in the background. He winked at me when we formally shook hands. Silly, really, but that was the way Mui had set it up, that was the way she wanted it, so we played along. I felt like a puppet. After all the commotion was over, I had to go back to my car to pick up my suitcase. Louis came with me. The darkness made our walk companionable; we had a bit of a laugh, and our conversation was easy.

A wine glass was added to the table when we returned. We talked for another hour about Louis' trip, his stop in Washington, meeting President Kennedy, who had been standing in an open car, stopped by the crowd surrounding it. Louis told us he had a great photo of him on his Hasselblad camera, the same type of camera left on the moon at the first landing. I was briefly talking about my presentation at Marburg University when Louis started yawning. The time difference and the release of tension of meeting me for the first time had finally caught up with him. We got up and said goodnight. Before going to my room, I went into the large guest room with Louis because I wanted to take a look at little Isabelle. I was shocked. I saw a different child, not the sweet little Bella of the pictures and my dreams. All her golden locks were gone, she had an unflattering haircut with hair straight as chives. There was nothing of the cuteness that made me fall in love with her. I must have been looking at Louis with my mouth agape.

"Everybody thought short hair would be better for the trip. The curls were still Bella's baby hair. Now she looks more like a Kindergarten girl at her four years of age."

I was disappointed. What an awful haircut! I would take her to a good hairdresser, the first chance I'd have. My hairdresser would exclaim, 'My God, where did she get that haircut? At 7-Eleven?' I was wise enough not to say anything to the proud father about my feelings or intentions.

Breakfast at the Baders was always at 9.00 AM, no matter what. At 9.00 AM, everybody had to appear showered, the hair brushed, and fully dressed. Vati always wore suits and tie. Mui would wear a lovely dress with colour-coordinated jewelry. I loved the sumptuous breakfast: a variety of bread, buns, cheese, cold cuts, smoked ham, honey and at least two types of jam and marmalade. Oh, don't let me forget the obligatory boiled egg. All meals at the Baders had set meal times: lunch (the main meal) at noon, tea at four and a light dinner at 6.00 PM. The German tradition is to 'breakfast like a king, lunch like a prince and dine like a pauper.'

    The conversation flowed smoothly. Bella sat between Louis and me. She was very quiet, not able to speak or understand German. Mui tried her English on her, Bella looked at her but said little, just nodding or shaking her head. I mainly smiled at her, and she must have realized I couldn't speak her language, poor kid. But I helped her get her food, she would point, and I would nod and say, "it's good, hmm?" Louis was her saviour. After breakfast, the three of us went for a walk, we held her hands between us, took short runs and swung her up every few steps. It made her laugh, and she asked for more. Louis told her to speak very slowly to help me understand her. Somehow, it worked. For the rest of the day, she never left my side, always holding my hand or leaning against me.

FLIGHT INTO THE UNKNOWN

6: WEDDING BELLS

As luck would have it, my next lecture tour promoting the idea of skincare from the inside out brought me back to Augsburg. The company I worked for produced health and skincare products based on the unique wheatgerm discoveries of my boss, Dr. Grandel. Working with their chemist, I had been instrumental in developing their first skincare line. I told Dr. Grandel about our wedding plans and my impending emigration to Canada and gave three-month notice. He was very understanding but did not like the fact my parents would not be at the wedding, and my sister from Hamburg did not want to come. She had two small children but also thought she would not fit in with the Bader family. I dared to ask Dr. Grandel,

"Would you consider attending my wedding and be my witness? Otherwise, I have nobody from my side, neither family nor friends."

"I'll be proud to come. You and I will go shopping and pick out a wedding present for you. Would you prefer a Rosenthal china set for twelve or rather something personal, like jewelry? Don't answer me now, sleep on it, we can decide tomorrow."

The company always booked a room for me in the five-star 'Hotel Drei Mohren' when I was in Augsburg. Since the receptionists and waiters knew me, it felt a bit like coming home. Sleep eluded me that night. Had I anticipated problems with the company? Did I think or perhaps hope they wouldn't want me to go, and Dr. Grandel would try to talk me out of it as well? The next day I let him know that I prefer a personal gift and not any household items.

"I was hoping you would say that. Come, let's go to my favourite jeweller in the city."

Dr. Grandel, known at the jewelry shop, was greeted like an old friend. He told my wedding story and asked to see lovely bracelets. I had two necklaces, a double row of cultured pearls and the gold chain from Dr. Bader with the little globe pendant. I had no bracelet. They placed a black velvet tray with a dozen beautiful bracelets in front of me. I picked the one I thought was probably the least expensive. Dr. Grandel shook his head and exclaimed,

"No way! Don't be shy. That one is not good enough. It's more suitable for a young girl. I think you should get this one. It's heavy; it's different. If you don't like it in Canada, you can sell it. It's your insurance so you can come back home. You know, your job is always here for you."

"Thank you, but I…" I choked up and looked at him with tears in my eyes.

He left me no choice. Did I want another option? No. I liked the heavy feel on my wrist. I also wanted to please Dr. Grandel. He chose it. It was the most expensive one. The design was different than any I had ever seen. It consisted of several strings of white gold, strings of red gold, and strings of yellow 14-carat gold. It weighed close to 90 grams. What a gift!

As if that wasn't enough, Dr. Grandel took me to a fairytale toy store and picked out a fancy doll for little Isabelle since I might be in Canada for Christmas. We finished the shopping spree in a crowded café looking out at the Rathaus (city hall) Plaza.

He proudly told me about the city hall. It had been destroyed by bombs as was most of the 2000-year old city. Based on photographs donated by the citizens, it was rebuild in the original Renaissance style of the late 1700s. The problem had been the targeted infamous Messerschmitt factory; it was just a few kilometres away.

The company tentatively accepted my resignation for the 1st of January, 1964, pending the approval of my immigration papers. Dr. Bader started the process and assured me I would not encounter any problems since I would be married to a Canadian citizen. I had to go through extensive health check-ups, and the test results sent to the Canadian consulate. The same would apply to Louis intending to marry a German girl. As soon as he arrived, he had to start the process, or the wedding could not take place. One of the tests included proving his fertility. It did not matter that he was the father of two children. The test results were late; the wedding needed to be postponed until the 25th of October.

I had looked forward to Dr. Grandel being my witness and be at my side on my father's behalf. What a disappointment when he had to cancel because of other commitments on the new date. Did his gracious gift make up for him not being at my wedding? No. I felt entirely alone in the extended Bader family. I would have to leave Germany after my marriage. I would have felt safer with Dr. Grandel there. How I wished my parents could have come - or at least my dad. I was overwhelmed by the Bader family; they had arranged everything without even asking me. I had nobody to lean on to lend support. I didn't even realize how much I needed it.

Louis and I had exchanged many letters to plan his time in Germany and for me to start buying things to take to Canada. He owned practically nothing for a household. Louis had left their house, and everything in it, to his ex-wife. Living in room-and-board, he did not need anything. He told me to buy what I liked. I had to make arrangements for a container, find buyers for my car, my possessions, and a new tenant for my apartment. There were six applicants for my residence, and a lady slightly older than me would even buy every piece of furniture. She insisted on being the first on the waiting list and left a down payment. Louis sent a registered letter with a money order made out in my name for 800 Deutschmarks, money for his expenses in Germany. He hoped we could visit Berlin where he grew up, and for our few days of a honeymoon, I had suggested Rothenburg ob der Tauber, my favourite romantic town in Germany. Louis loved my suggestion. Rothenburg, located along the Romantic Road on top of a mountain, is surrounded by a wall with four gates.

Before the critical date, I still had a lecture in Kiel/Holstein in the far north of Germany. It was a very long drive from Augsburg in the south. Thank God for the Autobahn, one of Hitler's good ideas. I don't think anybody can imagine Germany without the Autobahn. No speed limits, just a recommended maximum in specific areas. I had never been to the city of Kiel, the gateway to the Baltic Sea. Dr. Bader was born in Kiel. It wasn't surprising that he had joined the Navy. What a lovely harbour with so many ships, small ones, large ones, even the famous tall ship, 'Gorch Fock,' was present. It was now a noted German Navy training ship for sailing, simply called the German School Ship.

Young Dietmar had already made up his mind; he would train on that very ship. I took my time sight-seeing. I still didn't have a dress to wear on my wedding day. As I passed a shop window, one caught my eye, a plain cotton lace on white silk lining, a simple cut, lightly modelled to the figure, no sleeves and covering the knee. It would be perfect since I could later wear it as a cocktail dress. I tried it on; it fit as if made for me. I bought it. I loved it. Next, I looked for shoes. I found a pair with rather high heels perfect with the dress. To wear them for the wedding would be all right, but later? Probably not, they were not comfortable. A lingerie shop was my last stop. I had my complete wedding outfit.

On my way back to Wiesbaden, I stopped for a day in Hanover to finalize the sale of my apartment. How lucky I was, the buyer bought all my furniture except the few items I wanted to keep. I arranged a meeting with the overseas shipping company Kühne & Nagel for a preliminary estimate. I started to get the jitters. My God, it was happening. Somehow, I felt like an actress in a movie, and I was playing my part.

The Bader family was relieved to see me back, this time on holiday. Little Bella wouldn't let go of me. I was quite emotional to see how happy she was to have her new mommy by her side. She must have missed me. With his usual grin, Louis gave me a list of the items we still had to do for my emigration. We got it all done within the next few days. He expressed his wish to visit Wuppertal; he had been apprenticed as a carpenter there after the war. He was fifteen when he and his whole class at the boarding school received the dreaded conscription and the order to report for war duty in Frankfurt. They only had a week of training before being dispatched to Hanau and assigned as anti-aircraft gunners shelling the bombers flying over this area. He was not a strong, healthy boy; the stress, the cold, and the wet weather caused him to come down with pneumonia. He was placed in a field hospital and missed the direct hit that wiped out his whole class in the trenches. He felt guilty to this day that he lived while all his school buddies

FLIGHT INTO THE UNKNOWN

had died. The war ended not long after this. Since he had not finished school, all he could do was learn a trade. Louis had completed only one year of training before moving on to a well-paying office position in a large company. Now, back in Germany for the first time after seven years, he wanted to visit some of his old friends and see the carpenter again. I suspected he wanted to get away from his parents and give us a chance to get to know each other better before the wedding.

I was tired of racing along the Autobahn, but we still made the Wuppertal trip before the wedding, which was just two nights away. There were no fireworks that night as we slept together for the first time. Was it all part of my actor's script? I still remember the look on Louis' face when he came from his shower and joined me in bed with that silly grin of his. He apologized for not even being a 'minute man'- but it had been years since he... I did not blame him; I didn't know any better anyway. I only knew from romance books it could or should be something incredible.

A few days before the big day, Mui took me aside and confessed she had seen my new white dress and the shoes in my wardrobe.

"It's bad luck to buy yourself a wedding dress. You shouldn't have, but I know you are very independent, and your parents couldn't do it for you. You probably don't know it is not acceptable to wear a wedding dress without long sleeves. Vati's two cousins and I have decided to buy you a veil. Since you bought a short dress, it has to be a short one, covering your shoulders. Don't tell me you don't want one, we bought it, and I'll dress you, and you will like it."

"Why would you want to dress me?"

I had never thought of that. I felt uncomfortable at the thought of Mui helping and criticizing me for sure.

"No arguments! You don't have your sister here, so I'll do it. A bride needs help."

And that was that. On my wedding day, she turned up in my little room. I had to take all the needed items, and she took me to her dressing room upstairs. Luckily, I had put on my underwear already.

"Wonderful," she looked me over; "Louis will like to take that off you. Make sure, my girl, give him a night to remember. He had so much heartache with his first wife…"

I interrupted her before she went any further.

"It won't be a night to remember. I have my period."

On this day of all days, I didn't want to hear anything about his first wife.

"Oh, my dear God, poor Louis!"

She stared at me, shocked. She had no idea poor Louis knew about this already. I had mentioned it briefly during a conversation when I complained about my monthly headache. He had been compassionate and hoped I wouldn't suffer too much.

"We have the rest of our life to make up for it."

I got dressed in my blue suit with a yellow rose and forget-me-not corsage and a yellow silk blouse for the civil ceremony at the Mayor's office. A bouquet of yellow roses mixed with blue forget-me-nots was in a vase on the table. After Louis had signed the papers, I stopped with pen in hand for a few seconds before I signed my new name and looked at my father-in-law. He knew what I was thinking. I was reluctant and would have liked to back out of this. Talk about getting cold feet! He nodded to me with a little smile and quietly said, trying to make it sound like a joke,

"Remember, you'll never find another father-in-law like me."

The witnesses and the officer laughed, and I signed. We drove home in Vati's black Mercedes. I changed into my wedding dress with Mui's help; she placed the veil on my head and presented me to Louis. He handed me a bouquet of salmon-coloured roses. He wore his black suit, joked about it and called it his 'multiple wedding suit.' Then we were off again in the black car to the Marktkirche in Wiesbaden for the church ceremony I had requested. Louis had agreed to have Bella christened since her mother didn't have religious beliefs. All the guests were to meet us there.

Granny, Louis' mother, had brought her granddaughter Bella. They were waiting for us in the community room with rows of empty chairs since our wedding party consisted of only eleven adults and the two children, Dietmar and Bella. A severe disappointment awaited me. It was a dreadful surprise to find the beautiful church closed for extensive restorations. The wedding ceremony and Bella's christening were to take place in the drab community room. I could have cried. I felt as empty as the surroundings. Was it bad luck that I had bought myself a wedding dress? It looked and felt all fake.

We all drove to the lovely hotel in Bad Schwalbach, not far from the Bader's home, for the noon meal. It was veal schnitzel in a cream sauce, cauliflower with hollandaise, salad, dessert, and white wine. After lunch, we met up in the family's living room. Everybody wanted to celebrate and was talking at once, and everyone wanted to know what Louis had planned for us in Vancouver. Bella learned to smoke and drink champagne, taught with love by her Granny. Granny had given me a beautiful necklace as a wedding present. The platinum chain with the delicate pendant with thirty-eight small diamonds and a large sapphire in the center had been in her family for several generations.

"Oh, Granny," I was fighting tears; "I'll treasure this and pass it on to Bella on her wedding day," knowing how much she loved the girl.

"No," Granny answered, "you keep it and wear it as long as you want to, even if you are in your seventies like I am now. If you have no children with Louis, leave it in your will to Bella. She will be too young when she marries; she might not fully appreciate it or be able to keep it safe for future generations. I know you will. You are a lot like me, and you appreciate tradition. I know your family has lost everything and has no heirlooms to pass on to you. You and Louis will start a new life, and I hope a new family in Canada. May this be your connection between your old and your new family."

By now, my tears started to fall freely. I hugged the old lady, and, when she wasn't busy with her beloved granddaughter, she held my hand for the rest of the afternoon since we sat next to each other. She mentioned the diamond collier she was wearing would go to one of her daughters in America.

The hours flew by, and soon Louis looked pointedly at his watch to remind me we needed to get going if we wanted to arrive in Rothenburg ob der Tauber before dark. We had booked a two-night honeymoon stay, and then we would spend three nights in

Berlin before Louis flew back to Canada. He wanted to show me the famous Kurfürstendamm, the area where he had grown up.

Bella was sad she couldn't come with us, but there were many distractions for her with all the new aunts and uncles and Granny, and they all spoke reasonable English. She was a little tipsy from the champagne tasting and didn't notice our leaving. Our suitcase was already in my car, so we went the French way, meaning without saying goodbye.

Louis was relieved to flee the family stress. He was happy to be alone with me on the road. He loved Rothenburg. We stayed in the 'Hotel Goldener Hirsch.' Red roses were on our table, a fruit basket in the room and a glass of champagne served with the orange juice for breakfast. Louis felt like giving up Berlin. But we couldn't do that since the airline tickets were sitting on Vati's desk.

Bella hugged each of us hard when we came back. Mui had prepared her for another goodbye when Vati took us to the Frankfurt airport for the flight to Berlin the next morning. I packed my wedding dress, now a cocktail dress, since Louis wanted to take me to 'Resi'- a dancehall he remembered. We didn't know if it had been bombed or still existed. After a day of walking through the bombed-out Berlin, we had a leisurely evening meal, changed and excitedly went to the damaged but still operational dancehall. It was interesting. I had never been to a place like this, mostly two-seater tables, each having a large number and a small telephone on it and a pneumatic pipeline. One could send a note or an invitation to dance to another table by dialling the table number. Louis excused himself while I sat alone at our table. I knew I looked stunning in my white dress with a single red rose pinned upside down on my left chest, Granny's necklace around my neck, and the Dr. Grandel bracelet on my wrist. I studied the people at the other tables, sometimes two men or two women, not always couples. Many were looking around to find a dance partner. I caught quite a few glimpses of men checking me out, but I had my right hand with my shiny wedding ring visible on the table. The sound I heard when a message arrived through the pipeline startled me. There was a note. My heart went crazy. Who would send me a message? It said:

"Madame, you are beautiful."

FLIGHT INTO THE UNKNOWN

I looked around to see if I could make out the man who might have sent it to me. That moment a smiling Louis came back. I discreetly showed him the note and expressed curiosity regarding the sender.

"Didn't you recognize my writing?"

Wow! I was glad for just the candlelight in the room. Then I laughed,

"Fooled you! But quite a few men gave me the eye when you were gone."

"I was afraid of that. I'm glad nobody asked you to dance. May I...?"

He was a good dancer. For three hours we danced every dance. They played all the oldies of the fifties. I had not danced for a few years, but I loved dancing and enjoyed myself. I think it was here where our bonding started, swaying and whirling to the beautiful music in this semi-dark room with only the candlelight illuminating it.

The next day, we walked to the street where he had lived with his family before evacuation. His father had fought in the war as a naval commander. Louis almost cried as we stood in front of a tall pile of bricks and debris. We even climbed onto the pile and looked at the surroundings. Once upon a time, this was the house he grew up in until he was seven years old and sent to the boarding school, a former fort-like castle in Nordeck. His two sisters and his older brother had already been there for a few years. His mother joined them when the bombing in Berlin was nightly. In Nordeck, they all lived in one room with Mr. and Mrs. Vogel, a sweet elderly couple. The castle had been converted to a hospital for all the wounded soldiers, except for one schoolroom. Nordeck wasn't quite the calibre of Salem or Eton, but all the kids were from well-to-do families. Louis' best friend was the son of the Agfa family, Agfa being the German equivalent of Kodak. Their home was a castle in the Spessart Mountains. Louis had often spent his holidays with them. His friend had a darkroom at home, and Louis learned all about photography and developing the pictures. Those skills served him well in Canada. At present, he worked in a large laboratory, being responsible for the installation of new colour photo developing machines, getting them functioning and training the people working on them.

While standing on this massive pile of rubble, my memories went back to the nights in 1943, 1944 and 1945 when we were sitting or lying in a ditch about a hundred meters from our house, watching the bombers flying over us like angry hornets. We children tried to count the dancing phosphor bombs in the sky. We stared and shivered to see the night sky turning red, night after night when all those mad hornets flew to empty their bellies over Berlin. It was only fifty kilometres (as the crow flies) from us. One night, the sky had been unusually bright red; the fire seemed so close as if it was right behind our mill hill. We knew it was the burning city of Berlin. I had previously visited Berlin, I had seen the devastation, accepted the rubble as a leftover of WWII, but I never had a close personal connection to it. Now I was deeply touched by observing Louis. He cried for his lost childhood and all that was or could have been.

A police officer looked up to us. He demanded we come down immediately.

"Did you not see the warning sign of unexploded bombs or grenades? It is verboten to climb these piles of rubble."

No, we hadn't paid attention. Louis explained this pile of rubble was once upon a time the house he grew up in, he was visiting from Canada, and he had longed to see it. He apologized for having overlooked the warning sign.

"This pile of rubble would have been our grave if we had been here, trapped in the cellar. The evacuation saved our lives."

The officer was compassionate and told us some heart-wrenching stories about families who still might be under some of those piles of rubble. It would take a long time to reconstruct Berlin.

He accompanied us to the Gedächtniskirche, a memorial church at the corner of the Kurfürstendamm, an empty shell with two half towers like hollow teeth, pointing at the sky. The officer told us about those bombing raids, how burning people had run screaming along the roads, looking for any body of water. But even jumping into a canal or river would not douse phosphor flames. The incendiary bombs, the dancing Christmas trees I had seen in the sky from our ditch in Pomerania many years ago, had killed the people who were able to crawl out from collapsed buildings or bomb shelters. I thought of Mrs. Dreger, a lady I worked with for a couple of years in Hanover. She had seen her parents burn and scream until they fell and died. She was unable to help them and could only watch. How horrible. The police officer told us this church would never be torn down or rebuilt to the glory it once was. The remaining walls and the towers would be stabilized and become a memorial of the terrible war.

  Louis flew back to Canada a few days later, and I went back to work. Before I knew it, it was December. It was time to book my flight with Bella to Canada. My company was very gracious in allowing me to leave earlier than anticipated. On the 14th of December, the Bader family drove us to the airport in Frankfurt. I am unable to describe the feeling of walking away from them and everything I had ever known. I felt their eyes on my back, but I never turned around for a last wave of goodbye. I would have broken down. Deep in my heart, I even had feelings of resentment and blamed them for this departure. No, I did not cry. It was as if this person walking away with a little girl on her left hand was not me at all. There was a bare grey cement wall on my right side without any decoration whatsoever.

FLIGHT INTO THE UNKNOWN

7: E-DAY - EMIGRATION DAY

With Bella's little hand in mine, I boarded an airplane at the Frankfurt Airport. When the plane lifted off, we watched the fields of Germany getting smaller and smaller. We admired the many little villages with the steeple church towers, always right in the middle of the surrounding houses. Bella said,
"They look like toys out of a building toy set."
The endless grey band of the Autobahn reaching out to the sky gave way to floating clouds. Then there was nothing. We were above the earth, above it all.
I had left the land of my ancestors. I was on the way to a new life on a different continent. Would I escape my troubles, my apprehensions, my sadness, the constant feeling of not being good enough and loss? It is hard, if not impossible, to explain what, or how I felt: weightless? Floating, like a feather in the wind? It had nothing to do with flying. I am talking about my emotions, my feelings, even my physical body. When I drifted off into semi-consciousness, I had an out-of-body experience. I had no feelings; I had no physical body. I looked down at myself in the airplane seat, eyes closed with a crease between my eyebrows, hands folded in my lap. I did not want to come back to reality when I heard a small desperate voice and woke up.
"Lady, can I have a drink?" The voice of my new daughter. The four-year-old girl, cuddled next to me, knew I did not speak much English. She had not wanted to wake up her new mommy, and she was calling the stewardess. Bella couldn't sleep. Her dad

was waiting in Vancouver. Rolled around by wind and waves, she was like a pebble on the beach. Her mother had left her when she was only two. She lived with her dad in room and board for a couple of years and the last nearly three months with her paternal grandparents in Germany. When I visited on weekends, she wouldn't let go of my hand. She was desperate for motherly love and would proudly introduce me to anybody: "This is my new mommy."

Today was the 14th of December, 1963. We had a refuelling stop at the International Airport Keflavik in Reykjavik, Iceland. We didn't like the smoke-filled waiting room, so we got out and walked on the frozen grass of the airfield for almost an hour. Holding her little hand tightly in mine, we seemed the only people on the planet. We both giggled when we found a small bush and relieved ourselves, trying to hide behind it. Finally, they let us board the propeller plane again to continue the long flight to North America over the green fields and mountains of Iceland and the icy white peaks of Greenland, occasionally visible through the clouds.

Up until then, I had no idea that Iceland is green and Greenland is white. I have looked down on Greenland many times after that, and it always irked me when I could not see any green, just incredibly beautiful white peaks and valleys. It's hard to believe people live there.

Twenty-three hours later, it was still the 14th of December 1963, we arrived in Vancouver, Canada. The Vancouver International Airport was a shadow of what it is today. At that time, the Vancouver Hotel was the tallest building in the city. I was overwhelmed by the beauty, glimpses of the Pacific and the backdrop of the majestic Coastal Mountains. I was quiet, just trying to take it all in. Halfway across the Lions Gate Bridge, my Canadian husband asked me:

"Well, what do you think?"

"This place is too beautiful to live here. It is more like a holiday destination…"

He laughed. "You better get used to it. Because you will live here."

He had rented a two-bedroom townhouse on Plateau Drive in North Vancouver. I liked the place with the large picture window in the living room, overlooking a small flower bed with pansies in

FLIGHT INTO THE UNKNOWN

bloom and tulips ready to pop open at any moment. Imagine - in December! It was winter in Europe, and here were flowering plants? Unbelievable. Louis had bought second-hand furniture for the master bedroom and a bed and a dresser for Bella's room. I was awestruck when I saw the kitchen. It had everything, stove, a fridge bigger than I had ever seen, a counter with cupboards above and below, more counter space on the other wall with a window and a double sink in front of it, and more cabinets on both sides. I did not know a 'Lazy Susan' - but there was one in the corner. How would I ever fill all these spaces? In Germany, you had to buy your cupboards and appliances; and here they were included? The living room was quite bare. We had agreed to wait for my container from Hanover, due to arrive in March.

Bella and I were exhausted. We went to bed early. She was out like a light. It was more difficult for me to drift off since I expected Louis would want to make love, but he didn't, he let me sleep. He cuddled up to me the next morning, and nature took over. Somehow I didn't feel right about it, but he was my husband, it was his right. All of a sudden a little voice said,

"Daddy, don't hurt Mommy."

It was a shock for both of us. I pushed Louis off, Louis got mad and harshly commanded,

"Next time you knock. Get out of here. Close the door."

Bella looked deflated, shocked and was ready to cry. My feet were on the floor. I wanted to take her in my arms and rock her like a baby. I asked Louis quietly to let her come in and cuddle between us. After all, she was used to sleeping with her dad in one room when they lived in room and board. He wouldn't have it. He was disappointed by the interruption.

"She has to get used to it. She has her room now, we have ours, and she has to learn not to come in like that. Stop! I don't want you to go out to her room now."

It was an order. Louis had hurt my feelings. I thought Bella would learn, but not this way, slowly and more naturally. But, he was her dad, and I didn't want to rock the boat the first day we lived together. My gut warned me this was not the end of it.

After breakfast, we went out to shop for a Chesterfield and chair for the living room. We found a green set in a second-hand shop for $25.00. I cleaned it, it looked all right and was quite comfortable. It was news to me that a Chesterfield only came with one chair in Canada. I was used to having at least two or even three around the table. A friend of Louis offered to build us a cabinet with sliding doors in the middle and drawers on each side. I painted the bed and dresser in Bella's room, and we got her a small desk and chair. She loved to draw. Her favourite art topic was her new little family: Mom-dad-little girl in all kinds of settings. There was always a big yellow sun in the upper right corner.

E-Day. The 14th of December is my E-Day, an extraordinary day in my life. It's also my sister Christel's birthday and the birthday of her first daughter, Delia, my goddaughter. For me, the 14th of December is and always will be like my new birthday:

A new beginning in Canada, a new chapter of my life.

FLIGHT INTO THE UNKNOWN

8: NORTH VANCOUVER

It was probably a week after my arrival when the doorbell rang for the first time. Opening the door, I was looking at a man holding baskets in each hand, filled with lots and lots of different brushes.

"Tadah! I'm the Fuller Man!"

He lifted both arms to show off the brushes. I had no idea who or what a Fuller Man was. I looked at him uncomprehendingly and said slowly,

"My - man - is - not - home."

It was the first full English sentence I uttered in Canada. The Fuller Man's face showed surprise mixed with shock, and then a light went on in his head.

"Ah! Okay, I'll - come - back - at - another -time."

He spoke as slowly as I had, and he said something about Christmas. Since it was close to Christmas, I assumed he wished us a happy Christmas. Too bad, Bella wasn't at home. She was my little English teacher, and she would surely have done a super job conversing with the Fuller Man. My husband got a kick out of this when I told him.

Mortifee Munshaw, the company Louis worked for, held a staff Christmas Party. We attended, and many people welcomed me to Canada, including quite a few Germans. Several couples became our friends. We met for dinners in either their homes or ours over the next months. Louis' colleagues, who spoke English to me, were a bit of a problem. I got the gist of what they were saying, but I had trouble answering in the same language. I nodded and smiled my way through the evening, sometimes saying thank you when I felt it was right to do so. To be honest, at that Christmas party, I felt sad, dumb, even stupid and thought of Germany where I had been a somebody, smart and never short of an answer. On the contrary, with my wit and humour, people would crowd around me and always shared lots of fun and laughter.

A small dairy farmer family, friends of Louis, invited us for the Sunday before Christmas. It was about an hour's drive from North Vancouver. They were Germans, owned sixteen cows and had just installed an automated milking system, the proof of their success. They were proud to show us everything after the German custom of serving coffee and cake in the afternoon. Their dog got a command to bring the cows in from the meadow. Each cow knew her place in the barn. It was impressive. The prepared feed got the cows munching, and we watched as the milking machine was attached to the nipples of an udder. We saw the milk flowing through the clear plastic hoses to a shiny aluminum container. The farmer's wife explained it to Bella, who could not comprehend it. Holding tightly onto my hand, she asked quietly:

"Why do you have a machine making milk? I thought the cows make the milk."

The woman picked up a tall glass. She sat down on a three-legged stool next to a cow and told Bella:

"Watch me! I can get the milk out of the cow by hand. The machine is to make the job much easier for us."

She handed the full glass to Bella, she held it, scrunched up her face and uttered,

"Ugh, it's warm…" She stared into the glass. She smelled it but never took a sip. With a wrinkled nose and big blue eyes looking at the woman she declared,

"I like the milk we buy from Safeway much better. It doesn't smell."

At that moment, the cow lifted her tail and made a big waterfall. We stood on the walkway between the two sides with the stalls. Waste would fall into a gutter, running water cleaned it automatically. Bella watched a cow relieving herself and looked at us with a big surprise registering on her face,

"I didn't know cows make beer too…"

FLIGHT INTO THE UNKNOWN

We controlled our laughter in order not to hurt her feelings on this happy day. My first ever turkey dinner followed all the excitement before we drove home again. Bella slept. My God, how much I loved this little girl.

Before we knew it, it was Christmas Eve. Our first live Christmas tree was about five feet high. Decorations had not been expensive. We sat around the tree on the floor, and we unpacked a big parcel with welcome gifts from the grandparents. Something for the body, something for the soul, just like it had always been at my parent's home, but nothing had ever been this rich. I had brought the beautiful doll from Dr. Grandel for Bella. I still see her looking at me when holding it in her arms, and nothing else mattered anymore. I wish I still had all the photos Louis took that evening.

New Year 1964 arrived, and my husband happily told me he had received a raise. His salary was $372.00 gross a month before I came. The company graciously increased his pay to $375.00, now that he had a wife and a daughter. When he got the first paycheck, he noticed the tax deduction was more than before, resulting in less net. He was not so happy anymore.

My final payment from my employer was still in my account in Germany. The exchange was 4.54 DM per Canadian dollar. I wanted to save a bit of money for a rainy day. I had paid for practically everything we needed. I had bought various sundries from dishes to cookware, crystal glasses, fine china for twelve, material for curtains, bed and table linens and what-have-you, everything was in my overseas container. I could hardly wait for it to arrive. Our apartment would be quite pretty when everything was in place. I had bought the best available Pfaff sewing machine, and I could make all the curtains myself. It paid off that my mother had registered me for a sewing course when I was fifteen. Currently, I was using a borrowed sewing machine to fix the few torn sheets Louis had. It felt like life in 1947 in East Germany.

I was frustrated with my inability to freely converse with Bella and my kind neighbours, especially the English lady who had renamed me. She had asked my name, then said, 'Gigi, what? I'll call you Giselle.' One day I saw Bella with a little boy exploring the differences between boys and girls. I was upset, went out, pulled her panties up and took her inside, telling her that her daddy would talk to her when he came home. She was mad as hell that I made her come indoors. She screamed at me,

"I hate you! I hate you!"

I sent her to her room to wait for Daddy. She understood more German than we realized, but she never spoke it. I felt helpless and cried. I could not discipline her or explain anything. I was, after all, her stepmother, and I had no right. From this day on, I felt shy around her. Nobody had ever hated me, and I was genuinely hurt. I didn't realize I was dealing with a small child acting out. She was always persona grata and spoiled by being the primary person in our family. Had my parents been right? I started to feel homesick and questioned my decision to emigrate.

In January 1964, I received a rather large cheque from my German Pension Fund. My husband had convinced me to opt for a pay-out rather than to keep it for my old age.

"But I need to provide for my old age. I have not worked in Canada and never paid into a Pension Fund in Canada…"

"Until you are sixty and ready for a pension, you won't need it. You live in Canada, and God knows what will happen in Germany during the next thirty years."

I was glad to have money and wanted to open an account for myself to deposit this cheque. I told Louis I would like to go shopping and buy the furniture we needed for the living room.

"No," he told me, "we will pay off our debts with that."

"Debts?" I did not know we had debts. "What are you talking about, what debts?"

"Well, there are still three years of monthly payments for the car, and so far, I only have a down payment on the building lot. I had to apply for a loan to come to Germany to marry you. I had to increase it to have money to rent this place and buy what we needed until your shipment arrives."

I was astounded and felt sick. I was stuck. Was marrying this man the biggest mistake of my life? I realized my well-to-do in-laws blinded me.

The apple doesn't fall far from the tree? Hahaha! I trusted my father-in-law when he talked me out of my plan to fly to Canada to meet his son before I married him. 'Own a car and a building lot,' he wrote in his ad. Naturally, I surmised he had paid for everything. It had been the cute little girl who attracted me. And now she hates me? Louis told me that one of the replies to his ad had been from a lady who had written, 'I weigh 300 pounds, but I have saved one-hundred-thousand Deutschmarks.' He should have chosen her if he needed money so desperately. I wondered what his parents had told him about me. He had never asked about my financial situation. I surely wasn't in that league. I would never have agreed to marry him if I had known I was to be a cash cow, pay off his debts and also pay for him coming to Germany to marry me. Pay a man to marry me? Over my dead body! I was boiling inside – but what could I do now?

I cried my eyes out that night, and in the morning, I signed the check on the back, and my dear husband took it to his bank to do with as he pleased. He told me it still was not enough to pay off the car loan. I suggested selling the huge fancy 1959 Monarch with the crowns and buying a smaller car. At least he agreed to that. He got a used Ford Falcon.

For my thirtieth birthday in January, I received an unexpected gift: a small cute kitten. It was the most adorable thing, playful as all kittens are, and full of love. I called him Prince Eugen. He learned quickly to jump out of the living room window to do his business in the flower bed and come back the same way. Prince Eugen brought our family together and playing with him made us all laugh.

Louis took the remainder of his holidays in February. Bella stayed with his friends Gary and Helen, and we drove along the coast to California. What a beautiful drive! At one point, we drove through an old-growth forest. The size of the trees was incredible; one was so big the road was built right through it. When I saw the first orchards with lemon and orange trees, I yelled,

"Louis, stop! I need to touch the fruit! I can't believe it is real..."

For me, a girl who grew up in Pomerania with apple and pear trees, who had walked miles to pick unripe apples along a back road in East Germany to fight off starvation, this was an unbelievable magical paradise.

I saw lemon trees next to house doors, orange trees in the gardens. Did the people, living in this paradise, know how lucky they were? I didn't think so. Lots of fruit was rotting on the ground. We had another experience, a quite scary one. Driving over the Sierra Nevadas, the road climbed higher and higher, got narrower with snow on the ground, with a steep mountain on the right, and an endless abyss on the other. There was no room to pass if someone was coming the other way. I needed to take over driving because Louis got a bad case of altitude sickness. Once over the mountains into Utah, we stopped for a break. I saw funny looking trees, and I ran towards one for a bit of privacy. I almost stepped on a big snake, curled up in the sun close to a tree. I couldn't get back into the car fast enough; any natural urges forgotten. Joshua trees, we learned, are the only trees growing in the desert. And lots of cacti, but they were not in bloom yet. I didn't even know these prickly plants could bloom. I was like a kid in wonderland.

When my container arrived in March, our apartment looked quite classy. The red machine-made Afghan carpet, the wedding gift from my in-laws, complemented the green Chesterfield and armchair. My stereo cabinet with radio, record player and record collection of classics and ballroom dance music was my joy while I sewed curtains for all the rooms. I called the carpenter, who had built the cabinet, to make a large bookcase for my books. Once my container was empty, a neighbour asked me what I was going to do with it. If we didn't need it, could he have it? He wanted to make a garage out of it for his Volkswagen Beetle. We were glad not to have to dispose of it.

I had made good use of my time since January by enrolling myself in an English course at the YWCA in Vancouver. I graduated from the beginner's class with flying colours, and the advanced course was even more fun. While I worked in the apartment, I always had my Telefunken radio on to get used to the sound of the language. I felt better about myself. Since I only had elegant clothing, Louis took me to an Army & Navy store. I got my first pair of jeans, and a plain army-coloured blouse and low-heeled shoes. I loved the outfit. A family, next door to our townhouse complex, had a pony. Sitting on the dividing wall with a handful of hay, the pony always came to me. It would munch the feed, and I talked to it in whatever language. It probably didn't get much attention from anyone else. Bonding with the pony, I was starting to settle in.

FLIGHT INTO THE UNKNOWN

At the beginning of May 1964, I got the biggest shock so far. My husband was tired of being paid so little in Vancouver. Without my knowledge, he had applied for similar jobs in other Canadian and even US cities. Offers from Orlando/Florida and Winnipeg were promising. In Winnipeg, four company owners, two brothers and two sisters, needed a manager. They offered to pay for a flight to Winnipeg for an interview. Louis returned with a contract for $400.00 a month plus $200.00 extra for living expenses, more money than he had ever made. He was ecstatic. I broke down and cried. He raved about Winnipeg, a charming city with quiet treed residential areas and rents lower than in Vancouver.

By the end of May, we had sold most of our furniture. The Chesterfield set we had bought for $25.00 I sold for $30.00. I had paid $10.00 for a mirror, sold it for $20.00. Everything out of a second-hand store looked good in our apartment and was now worth a little more. A moving truck loaded the rest. Prince Eugen had disappeared, and all our calling and searching for him brought no results. I guess he didn't want to move to Winnipeg. I did not want to either, but I could not disappear.

Packed to the roof, we took off in the now much smaller car on our way to Winnipeg. I was very, very unhappy. While driving through the Rockies, my little girl asked her dad,

"Why is Mommy crying so much?"

I couldn't stop.

FLIGHT INTO THE UNKNOWN

9: WINNIPEG - THE PRAIRIE TOWN

It was an incredible journey. Canada is quite an astonishing country - it's endless. The Rocky Mountains with beautiful vistas! I was stunned by the mighty Fraser River deep down below the highway, narrowing at the famous Hell's Gate. The Spiral Tunnel, dug through several mountains on either side of the road with a Kodak Stop to take photos, was mind-boggling; we read area history on a large poster. We saw a train enter the tunnel on the right and watched it disappear. After about ten minutes, it came out on the left, having passed under several mountains. I expected it would be heading in the other direction, but no, it came out to go east, the same way we were headed.

We crossed the Continental Divide, also called the Great Divide somewhere along the highway: the River waters flow either west to the Pacific or east to the Atlantic, and even to the Gulf of Mexico. It was also the boundary between BC and Alberta.

We overnighted in a small motel located next to the impressive Lake Louise Chateau. I couldn't believe it had taken only one year to build it and opened in 1890. We wandered around, taking lots of pictures. I finally stopped crying. I was awed by the setting. Vancouver, as well as Winnipeg, disappeared from my mind. All that counted was the here and now: No tomorrow, no yesterday. We were admiring Lake Louise, surrounded by mountains and a bluish-white glacier; it must be one of the most beautiful sights on earth.

The day we arrived in Banff, we had driven through an area called Buffalo Park with live buffalos roaming around, free. We felt vulnerable to attack since the road was not fenced off - but the wild beasts stayed where they were and just looked up as we slowly drove by. For the first time, we saw authentic, lived-in teepees. They were quite tall, white or light beige; some had symbols painted on them. Not all indigenous Canadians live in these tents with poles sticking out at the top to provide an opening for the smoke generated by the fire inside. I still can't understand why rain or snow would not come in that way.

In 1964, Banff was a small but picturesque town with some hotels along the main street. The massive, impressive castle-like Banff Springs Hotel was built at an altitude of 4,000 feet high on the mountainside during the railway construction from east to west and opened in 1888. Banff is a famous ski resort. On our way to enjoy a dip in the Sulphur Hot Springs atop a mountain, we saw several large elk resting in the driveway of a family home. These massive animals wander the city streets and are part of the charm of Banff. People accept the danger and have learned to live with it. In one area, close to the edge of the forest, we spotted several mighty moose.

Soaking in the hot thermal sulphuric smelling water made us very tired. We slept well that night. I had overheard a woman telling the masseur in a curtained off area about a bear attack in her backyard. The masseur mentioned the large wounds in her back were healing well. Her injuries must have been gruesome. It caused a nightmare for me. What a country! Bear and moose, elk, buffalo and other critters I didn't even know yet. The largest animals I knew were horses, bulls, and cows. And they were tame, fed and used by us. I had a lot to learn about Canada. I couldn't wait to tell my father about all of it in my next letter.

As the highway slowly eased downwards, the views became wider. The mountains retreated to the background. I reminisced about my father's excitement when we had had a chance to immigrate to the province of Alberta in 1948. He had come back from the hell of Siberia after two years of hard labour, the only surviving person of the fit and healthy sixteen to sixty-year-old men and women the Russians had taken from our village in 1945. Dad had found us again through the Red Cross in East Germany,

FLIGHT INTO THE UNKNOWN

which was under communist control. He had wanted to go far away and leave Germany behind. Our mother had settled down again after the eviction from our home in Pomerania in 1945. She couldn't forget our three-week walk on the road to nowhere, next to the Russian war machinery on their way to victory in Berlin. She couldn't face another uprooting. She was frightened of immigrating to Canada; being surrounded by strangers in a country she thought was behind the moon with a different language and culture.

Who could have known that one day I would be the one living my father's Canadian dream?

The Province of Alberta was incredibly green. I had never seen such extensive hilly valleys with lots of cattle grazing, and no fences like in Germany. Did the cows know where their borders were? Or were the farms so large it didn't matter? I didn't spot any cowbells, prevalent in Bavaria. I also couldn't see any dogs herding them together. What about milking? Maybe they were all the young ones not ready for breeding before becoming milk cows? One could see so much of the highway now; it stretched towards the eastern horizon. We overnighted in a small motel in the middle of nowhere. They had a pool, and the three of us enjoyed a relaxing hour in the warm water, watched the sunset over the Rockies and had a simple but tasty dinner. Bella was complaining about sleeping in a queen-size bed. There were two of those in our room. She suggested Daddy could sleep alone, and she would sleep with me. We paid $23.00, including breakfast.

On the road again, we crossed another border. A sign warned 'You are leaving the Province of Alberta' and another read 'Welcome to Saskatchewan.' The land was flat as a plate as far as one could see.

Louis spoke like a teacher: "We have arrived in the Canadian Prairie, the breadbasket of the world. The farmers here grow mainly wheat. The Wheat Board in Winnipeg distributes and sells it all over the world."

This information instantly brought back a statement my German boss, Dr. Grandel, had made. He told me about it when I first talked about my emigration to Canada. One of his degrees was a doctor of agriculture. He had mentioned the monoculture in the

Prairies would cause many problems in the future with disease and bugs, and deterioration in the size of the wheat plant and grain.

A timid voice behind us, "Are we there yet?"

"No, Bella, we still have another two days to drive before we are in Winnipeg. Let's look for another motel with a pool, and we will have fun again, okay?"

We drove about 400 miles a day and always ended our drive around four p.m. The straight highway made a curve after every twenty miles. Louis smiled and explained,

"It was planned this way so that drivers won't fall asleep and watch where they are going."

Yes, I could see how essential curves would be if you drive this endless grey band through the flat country more often. Everything was new to me. I looked at the lonely farmhouses here and there, no villages like in Europe. I saw a few ducks, and I admired the incredibly blue cloudless sky and the glorious sunsets. Every so often, we took a break, getting out of the car to walk and keep the circulation going. I noticed some funny critters standing up straight as a stick. Noting the slightest movement, they disappeared.

"Those are Prairie dogs," we learned. Dogs? Bella laughed. Some striped ones were even smaller and quicker. The Prairie looked still and dead, but undoubtedly, it wasn't. I wrote this little poem that early June evening:

> "Wide open spaces, a high blue sky,
> the sign of the Prairies, clouds sailing by.
> The endless highway, no sign of life;
> Dead skunks or rabbits seen on the drive.
> Prairie dogs, standing up high,
> look at the cars that are driving by.
> No sign of life, even in them,
> Black dots for eyes in a thing like a stem.
> Indian country. No cowboys in sight.
> The Buffalos gone. Did they lose the right to roam this land?
> Time goes on, and still, there is
> lots of life in the grass-covered sand."

FLIGHT INTO THE UNKNOWN

The sign which had advised us 'you are leaving Saskatchewan' was replaced a few hundred meters further with one saying:

'Welcome to Friendly Manitoba.'

That evening we checked into a motel in Virden, a small village. Bella was happy. She had thought hardly any people were living in Canada and now enjoyed seeing people entering shops. Many nodded a greeting and smiled at us. Everybody was friendly. We bought ice cream cones and experienced something like civilization again.

We knew our destination was not much farther. Winnipeg was the capital of Manitoba; the population only about 200,000. We started to see more cars, and the slogan on their license plates was 'Friendly Manitoba.' We talked about it at length.

We entered Winnipeg in the late afternoon on the 4th of June 1964. We drove along Portage Avenue, the long road from the west through the city, which connected to the Trans-Canada-Highway # 1 continuing east towards Toronto. We checked into a motel, bought some sandwiches and soft drinks for an in-room picnic, and settled for the night. I was apprehensive about what would happen next. What would life be like in 'Friendly Manitoba?' What I had seen so far reminded me of cowboy movie settings in California. I hardly slept, but Louis was happy, looking forward to his job and finding a place to live. He could hardly wait to start working again.

Louis bought the Winnipeg Free Press newspaper and marked several places listed for rent. We were lucky. The third one we looked at was on Dorchester Avenue, an upper duplex apartment with two bedrooms, a den, a kitchen and a good-sized living room. We even had our own basement. The rent was $110.00 a month plus utilities; we looked at each other and nodded. Yes, we wanted to rent it. We went shopping for a couch and two chairs. They were the new Danish Style. The sofa was reddish-orange, one chair was green and the other blue. Before buying anything else, we wanted to wait for our moving truck to arrive with our belongings, especially the bedroom furniture. We stayed three nights at the motel and then moved into our new home.

10: SETTLING INTO ORDINARY FAMILY LIFE

Louis started his job. At the company, located downtown, parking was limited. I offered to drive him and have the use of the car during the day. I was now an ordinary housewife. I scrubbed floors and walls and cupboards, cleaned windows, painted and made the basement approachable. I organized our dishes and clothing, went shopping with Bella and cooked meals. We checked out the school where she would start Kindergarten in September. We had a single garage full of spider webs, dust, empty cans, and other junk. I had to wear a shower cap and a surgical mask to attack it. Our half of the backyard, divided by a low picket fence, was overgrown with grass and weeds. I made a small flower bed along the divider as well as along the wall of the house. Bella and I went to a nursery and came home with marigold and pansy plants. I let Bella help me with the planting and, when finished, she was proud of our efforts. We did everything together. She corrected and helped me with my English, and since we spent most days alone together, we became very close.

During my few months in Vancouver, Louis and I had regularly attended the monthly German Movie Night. The organizer sent out a little two-page program with ads placed by German shops or businesses. In Winnipeg, we only learned about the German Movie Night through the local German Newspaper. I asked the organizer if I could put together a similar program for Winnipeg. He liked the idea. Bella and I visited one German shop after another. There were quite a few since Winnipeg had a substantial German-speaking population. The price for an ad the size of a business card was $30.00. Bella often got a little treat; she became fond of Gummy Bears. My commission was $5.00 for every ad I sold. It started slow, but soon I was making $30.00 a month. The two-page program doubled in size to four for the December issue. The last page, called 'Buntes Winnipeg Kaleidoskop' (Colourful Winnipeg Caleidoscope), was reserved for a letter from me to the movie-goers. I wrote about what I had seen in the shops, about specials, and about German lawyers, accountants, or other professionals I had met. I always had tips for healthy choices and signed my page with,

'Enjoy a few happy hours. Go to the movies…'

In the December issue, I wrote about the history of the Christmas tree. People loved it. I still have that page. Our life became routine. Bella was always at my side. One day, I prepared a meal with boiled eggs in mustard-sauce. When I was peeling the eggs, she suggested,

"Mommy, why don't you peel the eggs first and then cook them?"

On weekends the three of us explored Assiniboine Park with the zoo, Kildonan Park with old trees, ponds, and flower beds and even drove out to Grand Beach. Louis joined the German Club, and as a result, we started to get invitations to visit other German families. Bella was happy to play with children her age, kids who not only knew German but also spoke English. Summer 1964 was a laid-back affair, but we bonded as a family and enjoyed becoming part of a community. We got to know more neighbours and often talked about how friendly the people of Manitoba were.

For a special Sunday dinner, Louis invited his four Jewish bosses, two brothers and their two sisters. One of the men, George, was on holiday in Israel, and one sister had other obligations. Bella listened to the conversation, and suddenly asked,

"What is Israel?"

Moe explained, "That is the country where Jesus came from."

Everybody looked at Bella. "Oh, is Jesus there on holidays too? Will George meet with him?"

Bella was not raised with religion. I was not in any position yet to introduce Jesus' history to her. Moe was kind and explained,

FLIGHT INTO THE UNKNOWN

"No, dear, George won't be able to do that. Jesus is in heaven with God, His Father. Jesus lived almost two thousand years ago."

"Oh! I didn't know that."

It was a memorable evening. Louis had worked for the company for a few months but felt he could not yet fully exercise his expertise. During dinner, he tried to outline his plans for their company as he had not had a chance to do it at work. They liked his ideas, but the four bosses caused many problems during the following year by not being able to agree on anything. Louis was frustrated and grumbled at home. One day he hit me with the news he had given notice.

I almost fainted. What are we going to do? No income, in a city with no family or close friends, with a Siberian type of winter, rent to pay and groceries to buy; how could we survive? We knew his parents would not help. His father had admitted happily financing Louis' divorce and his second wedding but had pointed out, "Now that you are a family man, you are responsible for your new wife and daughter."

Louis applied for a job at the only competition to no avail. He decided to open his own business. I still had money in Germany, and he demanded I have it transferred. This transaction cut me off from Germany entirely, no chance to return, no money of my own to fall back on. Raised the old-fashioned way, I believed I had no choice but to obey my husband. Because of my money, he got a bank loan. We had new debts, and I prayed to God to help us make a success of the new business.

Louis found a suitable place on the corner of Ellice and Sherbrook. I scrubbed and painted, he made plans for dividing walls and water installations, darkrooms and an office, and he ordered the equipment needed. He found tradespeople and even a couple of employees. I was the receptionist, secretary, bookkeeper and Girl Friday, as well as the cleaning woman on Sundays. Bella was in Kindergarten. I drove back and forth between our home, office and school several times each day. A couple of months later, we opened Aetna Photo Laboratories Ltd.

The business made a good start. Louis was already well known in the professional photographer's fraternity. Quite a few fellows brought us their business. One, a German photographer, had recently opened a photo studio within the Hudson's Bay Store.

He offered a free portrait to all employees. They loved it and lined up. One of the ladies didn't smile. Try as he may, he couldn't get her to relax. Finally, he said,

"Come on, lady, show us your nipples!"

Roaring laughter followed that statement. What the photographer had meant was dimples - but it had the desired result. He became one of our best customers.

We advertised developing and printing for amateur and professional photographers. We offered specials on enlargements for Christmas. We made a splash when we offered personalized Christmas cards with 'your own photos and message.' To say we were busy is an understatement. Not only did I have a fulltime job (without pay) along with being a housewife and mother, but I started bringing files home for bookkeeping as well. Often, when Louis went to bed after a tiring day, I sat late into the night doing the paperwork. I also kept my movie program going. It was my only personal income, sometimes $25.00, sometimes $30.00 a month.

A lady with a couple of small kids lived across the street from our upper duplex apartment. I would go and talk to her whenever I saw her in her garden. I loved their old house. She was married to an opera singer, William Thiessen. His family owned the Grey Goose Bus Lines. Anita invited me to a coffee afternoon with her German-speaking lady friends, mostly Mennonites. All attending wanted to know more about my life. When they heard I had been giving lectures about healthy living and skincare from the inside out in Germany, one asked me,

"Would you be able to speak at our next Church meeting?"

They belonged to a Mennonite Church. I didn't even hesitate and said yes. After my first lecture, I received more invitations to speak to different groups. I was busy with my husband's business, but this was like dessert for me. I loved it. I had been missing it more than I realized. When I struggled for an English word, someone provided it. I learned a lot during these informal meetings, and we had many laughs. There was not much to laugh about at home. I was overworked, always stressed, and tired. Under the blanket, I often cried myself to sleep from pure exhaustion.

FLIGHT INTO THE UNKNOWN

11: ROLLERCOASTER YEAR - 1965

Towards the end of January 1965, we received a phone call from Toronto. It was Aunt Anna, the lady in Germany who had taken in Doris, Bella's younger sister. She was visiting, staying with a cousin. Aunt Anna's niece Kirsten, the mother of the girls, had remarried. Her new husband had three boys. Kirsten now wanted her daughter since she legally had custody of Doris. Aunt Anna was not sure yet if she would agree to it as she was afraid the boys would abuse her darling Doris. She promised to keep Louis up-to-date about further developments.

A couple of weeks later, she called again. She was upset, crying and emphatically stated she had to take Doris away from that family. There was no way she would allow her to live with them. It would ruin Doris for life.

"I am now sixty-eight years old. I cannot take my girl back to Germany with me. I am not able to care for her anymore. She needs parents; she needs a family. Louis, you have to take her! You have a sweet wife, she is good with Bella, and Doris will be happy to be with all of you. I know it will be tough for her not to come home with me. But honestly, I can't do it. My heart is breaking, but I have to give her up. And I cannot leave her with her mother. It's impossible. Please, please understand."

There was more. When Louis relayed all the information to me, I felt like a grenade had hit me; my life was organized by the minute. More now, again? Due to my heavy work schedule and the little time I now had with Bella, she had developed psychological problems, including bedwetting and seeing a psychologist. Losing her mother and baby sister in her early years must have been traumatic. Living with strangers, in her mind losing her dad when I entered their life, and now losing her new mommy to all the work, had a devastating effect on her. How could I take on another child?

When Louis still had his job, I had suggested we should try for a baby.

"It would cost us about $10,000. The government will not pay for the hospital birth; you have to be in Canada for three years before we become insured for that."

My doctor's prognosis put an end to my secret hopes:

"You will never have children. Your muscles are too tight, probably due to all your sports. Unless I do an operation."

I did not want an operation. Now, I was to take on another child? With her problems, torn away from her aunt, the only motherly person she knew? I was close to a breakdown. My husband told me he could not say 'no' because it is his daughter. I knew that, but I cried the whole night. Never in my life had I cried like that. I cried for all I had given up to be Bella's new mommy, to marry her father, who had not told me the truth about himself, and I cried for all I had to endure, for everything I couldn't have or do. When I had no more tears left, I made a pact with God. 'Please, God, give me strength. I promise to take on little Doris as my child.' Louis was relieved when I told him in the morning. I suggested seeing a lawyer to draw up a paper to sign the custody over to him so that Kirsten could never take her from us. I warned him:

"We can't run the risk of her changing her mind once Aunt Anna is out of the picture. We don't want to lose her again when she is part of our family."

It was done. Kirsten signed it. Aunt Anna wrote that everyone, even Kirsten, was relieved that Doris would grow up in a proper family. Bella was excited when we went shopping for a bed. We found one in a junky antique shop. It was an oak youth bed with a head- and a footboard. Bella begged to paint it pink. Doris' things arrived in an oversized parcel, including a doll carriage and twelve naked dolls. Naked! I made outfits for each one, even knitted little shoes and hats. All these babies sat along the wall on the pink bed in Bella's room. Bella was happy she wouldn't have to sleep alone anymore. She told everybody, "my little sister is coming soon."

The stress of that February had a terrible effect on Louis' health. His sensitive half-stomach had burst from bleeding ulcers. On March 17th, I drove him to an appointment for a checkup. I wasn't feeling well either. I could not keep my breakfast in, for no reason other than being a bundle of nerves. Louis came out with the doctor, who was going to give me instructions for his care. Dr. Campbell looked at me with a peculiar expression:

"Are you quite well? Please, come in for a moment."

Dr. Campbell was Scottish and to the point. He checked me and told me, sounding as if he couldn't believe it himself,

"You are pregnant."

I was stunned. I couldn't even get up. Tears were running out of my eyes, but no, I didn't cry. I couldn't help it. Pregnant now, with all that was happening? The nurse called Louis to come in again. That he was stunned as well would be an understatement as he reached for a chair. How would I ever be able to handle all my present responsibilities and everything coming? I closed my eyes and thanked God with a silent prayer. I was sure that HE knew how much this baby would mean to me, and it was HIS gift for me for accepting Doris as my own.

The next two weeks were probably the busiest of my life. A sick husband, a needy daughter, and me keeping the business running. Aunt Anna announced she would arrive with Doris on April 1st at 10:30 at night by train from Toronto.

What an April Fool's joke!

The baby in my tummy made me sick every morning. We kept the news to ourselves for now. I would have loved to shout it from every rooftop.

Bella was asleep when we drove to the train station to pick up Aunt Anna and Doris. The train trip from Toronto to Winnipeg had taken three days and nights. Both were exhausted. I crouched down in front of the shy little girl with her serious big brown eyes, holding on to Aunt Anna's hand, half hiding behind her. I told her how her sister Bella and all her dolls were waiting for her, and then asked her,

"Are you hungry? Would you like something to eat when we get home?"

She nodded. I asked, "What would you like?"

"Kartoffeln." (Potatoes)

Right. Doris did not speak English. I fried up a few leftover cooked potatoes. She did not want anything else. Aunt Anna and I readied her for bed. I was bending over her to tuck her in. Aunt Anna whispered, "say your prayer" - and, at that moment, Doris opened her mouth, and a fountain of very dry vomit went straight up into the air. I jumped back; I had never seen anything like it. She looked ready to cry, but, stroking her hair, I told her,

"Don't worry, it doesn't matter, I'll clean it up."

It was not a problem at all; it was so dry that it didn't even leave spots on the sheets. I could just shake it off into the bathtub. Aunt Anna suggested letting her sleep without changing the rest of the bedding. Doris was pale, her skin so white, and, with a shaky voice and compassion in my heart and soul, I said to Aunt Anna,

"It is all too much for her."

When I looked in on the girls in the morning, Bella was wide awake, but Doris slept. I put a finger to my lips and waved Bella out of the room. Incredibly, she had slept through all the commotion. She must have been physically and emotionally exhausted. Her sheets surely had to be changed. I was surprised when I found the same had happened to Doris. She probably didn't know how or where to find the bathroom or the potty under the bed.

Aunt Anna stayed for three days. Doris only left her side to play with her big sister in the basement. I had arranged a carpeted play corner for them. One girl spoke English, one spoke German, and they always understood each other. It didn't seem to matter. We were astounded. When they were alone, they chattered on. The day Aunt Anna left, Doris was very quiet, but did not cry. I sat down with her on our couch, one arm over her shoulder; I told her to come to me when she was sad. I will always be there for you, I promised, holding her hand. She did not respond or cuddle up. She was like a ghost with a broken heart and no tears. Poor kid, she was only four years old.

Within six weeks, she had picked up enough English to defend her timid big sister from neighbour's kids outside on the sidewalk. We stood behind the curtain at an open window and laughed. It was hilarious. Other kids did not dare to bully Bella when her sister was with her. And what was even more surprising: Neither wet the bed anymore, and Bella's emotional problems were also resolved. No more appointments with the psychologist. The kids were happy together; they had needed each other. I was relieved. They looked forward to the baby coming. They played baby with their dolls, and I had to make diapers for them. Once I overheard them praying for a sweet baby and begging God to make Mommy well again. Doris was used to praying before dinner, and before going to sleep. Bella suggested we should all do it.

After three months, I was well again and had more energy than ever. I was happy and got more done than I expected. The girls helped me with little things, for instance, bringing out the garbage and drying the dishes. We had good conversations as we worked together. They even learned to make their beds. On Sundays, we usually went to the zoo. I was able to take them to the beach at Lake Winnipeg a few times. My tummy was growing, and I tried to hide it with oversized T-shirts. Dr. Campbell did not want me to gain too much weight and allowed only one slice of toast for breakfast. I cut it into eight pieces and put something else on each bite and ate very slowly to make it last.

Louis reminded me of his cousin Karin, married to a millionaire in South America. I had met her sister and her mother, Freifrau von Estorff, at our wedding; we had liked each other. Her daughter Karin had married a sixty-year-old German-American when she was twenty-six. They had three children, the last one, a girl named Daphne, was born when he was seventy-six. I began corresponding with her, telling her about my baby and how hard we tried to build up the business. She wrote back,

"Do you mind if I send you my maternity dresses? They are like new. My mother told me you are my size. We finished with babies."

Wow! It was a gift from heaven. The dresses were expensive designer maternity dresses, and you couldn't even see I was pregnant. I looked like I had a few pounds too many, but otherwise elegant. They fit as if made for me. She sent us children's clothing as well, pretty little dresses. One day we received a more significant parcel with a collapsable car-bed, the size of a pram without the undercarriage. It would be handy to use as a crib until we could buy a real one.

At a craft fair, I won a baby-size Raggedy Ann doll, and I loved it. I named it Constance, after the magazine in which I had found the ad about Louis and Bella looking for a new mommy. I was dreaming of Constance Felicitas if I had a little girl, the names meaning the constant happy one. She would probably be called Conny. That was all right with me. I was alone with these dreams. Each of us had different ideas.

I prayed, "Please, dear God, let it be a boy. Let it be a boy, **please**.

My father's brother Curt was the last boy born into my family in 1909. My dad had always wanted a boy. He told us, "My wish to have a boy was the father of four girls." Later he insisted, "I am glad for my girls. At least they won't be cannon fodder for the next war." I wanted to make him happy by giving him his first grandson. I would name the baby after him since he would be born close to his birthday. I would call him Erich, actually, the English version of it, Eric. I would add Markus to it because Eric Markus sounded sophisticated and reliable.

My husband warned me: "I only produce girls. Don't get your hopes up."

The girls prayed: "Komm, Herr Jesus, sei unser Gast und segne was Du uns bescheret hast." (Come, Lord Jesus, be our guest and bless whatever you bestow upon us.)

Many things happened during the next few months. On a typical frigid November evening with the snow coming down in thick flakes, I felt weird when I went to bed; I woke up at 12.30 AM and just knew: This is it. I had nobody to ask how it would be or what to expect, but my body made it quite clear. The baby wanted to come and very soon. I shook my husband. He woke but turned around and yawned,

"It's probably a false alarm…"

The pains came every three to five minutes. We dressed, and I couldn't wait to get into the car and to the hospital. I was excited to soon meet this new little person. I grew wings and wanted to fly. With the thick blanket of snow, I did not trust Louis to drive; instead, I got behind the wheel of our Ford Falcon. He opened the garage door, and I backed out. Arriving at the exit of the back lane, I stared at a high snow windrow. No way of getting out. Looking at Louis, I uttered:

FLIGHT INTO THE UNKNOWN

"I hope the snowplow has not closed the other end of the lane."

I reversed up the entire lane, about a hundred meters, and hurray - we slipped out just as the mighty snowplow moved towards us.

Well, this was Winnipeg in Canada, known for its Siberian-like winters and heavy snowfalls. With our winter tires, we managed Wellington Crescent, not plowed yet, but made it to the Misericordia Hospital. We left the car in front of the entrance and hurried up to the desk. The nurse took one look at me, waved for a gurney, and off I went. I heard some terrible screams and thought, "I will not scream, no matter what."

The screaming was all around me while a doctor checked me. It was nerve-racking. I had to endure it for what felt like hours. In a kind of haze, I noticed I was wheeled away. Doctor Campbell, my doctor, was leaning over me and reassured me all was fine. I had horrible pains, but I promised I wouldn't scream.

At one point, feeling like I was submerged underwater, I heard his voice: "Give her gas, she won't make it." I thought he meant I would die.

The next thing I heard was him calling my name: "Giselle, wake up, wake up..."

Worn out, I did not want to wake up. I was too tired to open my eyes; I did not want to come back to all the pain.

Dr. Campbell kept calling: "Wake up, wake up... you have a son."

Somehow my brain registered the word. A son? Could it mean that everything was over and I was still alive? I risked one eye. Dr. Campbell held a bloody little something in his hands towards me, and it looked like a naked baby. I opened the other eye as well.

He repeated, proud as if it was all his doing, "You have a son."

This baby looked like a dried-up grandpa, my husband's father. I mumbled "red" and closed my eyes again.

"Don't worry," Dr. Campbell reassured me, "that's rust."

A nurse was busy cleaning me. As I was coming out of the fog enveloping me, I asked her not to tell my husband that I had a boy. She promised, "I won't."

I felt weak, but within me, there was an incredible feeling of all-encompassing love, it's impossible to explain. I was relieved it was over. Slowly my mind registered that I was now a real mother, the mother of a son. In the long hallway, a nurse wheeled me up to a man who had the most prominent, the stupidest grin on his face. It was my husband.

"We have a son," I told him with a weak voice.

His grin almost split his face in two. "I know," he smiled.

I felt deflated. I had wanted to tell Louis. I had wanted to see his face when he heard it was a boy. I whispered,

"Sorry, I know you wanted a girl."

"No way," he smiled, "I only said that so you wouldn't be disappointed. I knew you wanted a boy."

I looked at him, feeling disenchanted, and close to tears. The nurses had cheated me, and for some reason, I wanted to punish him. With a sideways look, I told him,

"Never again…" I meant sex. He didn't know.

"It's all right," he still grinned, "now we have three kids, that's enough."

I didn't say it out loud, but I was thinking, "Yes. YOU have three - I have one."

"At least I did not scream," I stated, just to say something.

"You? You screamed so loud I couldn't stand it. I had to leave. I couldn't remain in the waiting room. When I came back, I ran up and down, up and down this hall. Do you realize what date this is?"

I looked at him, quite disturbed.

"Today is November 19th. It took you twenty-five hours to deliver the boy. You screamed almost the entire time."

I shared a room with another mother. She had given birth to her third one. On the second morning, I couldn't wait for the nurse to bring my baby. She settled him in my arms for nursing. I had trouble getting him to latch onto my nipple. My nipples were too small, and they had given me artificial ones to place on top. I talked aloud to the baby.

"My goodness, how you have changed within this one day…"

The baby's head seemed different; his eyes closer together, his forehead was narrower.

FLIGHT INTO THE UNKNOWN

That moment the nurse raced back into our room. Red-faced and teary-eyed, she looked at me with another baby in her arms.

"So sorry, I made a mistake. I brought you the wrong baby. Please, do not report me, I'll lose my job. I was in such a hurry. Please, please don't mention it to anybody."

I was stunned. I let the nurse exchange the babies, and she left in a hurry. Oh, my God! The whole life of these two babies went through my head - what kind of people were the other parents? How would MY son have grown up - if not with us?

"I saw right away the baby wasn't yours," said the other mother. "I meant to tell you the moment the nurse came back."

My baby had red marks on his temples. During his next visit, I asked Dr. Campbell why. He explained he had to cut me and use obstetrical forceps to get him out since he did not want to do a Caesarian section. Then he told me the baby had to be circumcised. I was shocked.

"Why? Does that have to be? Is that necessary?"

It probably hurt me more than the baby. Louis had signed a form to have it done. Dr. Campbell explained the procedure was now done to boys at birth to save them problems later in life. That poor little dinky looked horrible, and I cried when I saw it the first time. I was upset, and Louis said it doesn't hurt the baby as much as it had hurt him when he had it done at sixteen years of age. The baby will not remember it. How would he know? I yelled,

"Just look at him. That doesn't hurt?"

I knew it was part of the Jewish religion and never understood the physical aspect of it. We were not Jewish.

After five days in the hospital, we could take baby Eric home and show him to the girls. Seeing their bright faces when I let them hold him, my happiness knew no bounds. The stairs to our upper duplex suite were my biggest problem. I was torn and cut severely, stitched up, and a nerve was damaged. I sat down on the first step and, with my arms and hands, lifted myself from one step to the next until I was upstairs. I did the same in reverse on the way back down to the basement to wash and rinse diapers. We had invested in a used wringer washer. We couldn't afford anything else. After a few days, Louis ordered a diaper service. I dreaded the bills, but it made my life easier. All I had to do now was rinse the diapers and keep them in a covered pail until exchange three days later. That was the way it was in 1965.

Louis' customers had been missing me in the office. When he explained I was in the hospital, they wondered and asked why.

"She didn't look sick. What's wrong with her?" Learning I had given birth to a seven-pound ten-ounce baby boy, they exclaimed:

"What? She didn't even look pregnant!"

Such was the effect of my one piece of toast for breakfast, and the designer maternity clothing from the South American cousin Karin.

Close to six weeks later, at about 2:00 AM, baby Eric would not stop crying. His crib was in the otherwise empty den. I was exhausted. Louis had admonished me to teach the baby to sleep through the night by not running to him every time he cried. But, like any new mother, I couldn't stand it. I snuck out of bed, tip-toed to the door when Louis' voice, rang out, loud and clear:

"You are not going!" It was an order.

For a moment, I stood stock-still and then I left. If Louis gets mad at me, so be it; the baby's crying sounded different. Upon entering the baby's room, I nearly had a heart attack. His little head was squished through and hung outside the rods of the crib; he was almost blue and would undoubtedly have died. I called out to Louis, he came running, and we had trouble getting his head back into the crib. Louis had turned down the protective side-covers offered when we bought the baby bed. After this shock, he came home with them the same day. It is wrong to save money when it comes to safety, even if you are as poor as church mice.

It was a hard time for us. During the first few years in Winnipeg, we sold many of my valuable possession to pay the rent and other obligations. Louis insisted on sending birthday and Christmas gifts to his two sisters in the USA. Because we did not have money to buy anything, he picked suitable items of my possessions. I never forgave him for it. Even several of the last gifts from my parents went that way.

"Look, we can live without that stuff, but we have to send them gifts." That was his excuse and explanation.

As soon as I could walk again, the doctor insisted I take the baby out for fresh air. We had no pram, and we had no money to buy one. I used Doris' doll carriage. We had wide sidewalks in our neighbourhood. People gave me funny looks; others stopped to see what I had in that tiny pram. Most of them were surprised; they couldn't believe it wasn't a cat or a small dog but a real baby. I usually smiled and said,

"In spring, we need a stroller, so why buy a pram right now for the few days it might still be possible to get out? There will be too much snow anyway."

On one of these outings, I walked by a stately house with four big white pillars. I stopped and stared at it. It was hard for me to believe that people lived in something like that. It was on Kingsway, a few streets over from Dorchester. I felt like in a dream, just as I had when I was in that Union Clubhouse in Stralsund. There I had had a feeling that I knew it, along with a weird premonition. I married later into the family who owned it. And now, little did I know that a few years hence I would live in this stately home.

Christmas 1965 was better for us than it had been 2000 years ago for the Holy Family, Mary, Joseph, and baby Jesus. We had a warm, nicely decorated living room, a lovely Christmas tree, German Christmas music on the record player. We were a happy, dressed up family with two pretty little girls playing with their dolls and me holding baby Eric for photographs.

After New Year's 1966, I had to go back to work. There was a lot of paperwork to catch up on, and lots of customers brought in their Christmas photo films. Karin had sent us a baby carry-cot, and it became Eric's day bed, sitting on my desk. He was a good baby, happy when he could see me or hear my voice and others around him. I did not have to worry about feeding or warming bottles since my milk was always the right temperature. I nursed him in the quite small and dark closet, pushing our winter coats aside. Those were precious, private moments. Our customers got used to it when they rang the bell, and all they heard was my muffled voice out of the closet in the corner,

"Just wait a minute, I'm going to be right out."

On Friday morning of March 4th, Bella went out the door to go to school. She was back after a minute:

"Mom, I cannot walk in that deep snow." Heavy flakes were drifting. A truck drove by. Louis took his daughter and put her in the tire track and told her to go to school. She looked so tiny, walking off into the white world. More than an hour later, a Chinese lady, who had a small convenience store close to the school, called us.

"If you are worried about your daughter, she is safe with me. I happened to look out of my door and saw this kid hugging a fence post, up to her shoulders in snow. I rescued her and gave her warm milk. If you want to pick her up, come soon. The blizzard is going to get worse. Did you not listen to the radio? You should never have let her go out."

No, we didn't have the radio on. We didn't know anything about a blizzard. Louis was at home because he had been preparing to go to the airport. He was unable to get a taxi. He went to pick up Bella.

We could have lost her. That blizzard was one of the worst Winnipeg had ever experienced. Five people had fallen and, in no time, were covered with snow. One was the sixteen-year-old granddaughter of a next-door neighbour out to get a Kentucky Fried Chicken. They found the dead when the snow removal started. Hundreds were staying inside the Eaton's and Hudson's Bay department stores. City buses were stranded, cars buried under the snow. People walked on top of them without realizing it. A snowdrift covered our entrance. We were grateful that a neighbour shovelled it away the next morning so we could get out. It was a sunny Saturday morning, and I was running out of baby food. We usually went shopping on Fridays, but that hadn't been possible. I got dressed warmly and tried to get to the Payfair store. With every step, I sank up to my hips into the snow. The Heinz baby food cans were in a paper bag, and it ripped. I had to dig them out of the snow and stuff them into my parka sleeves and pants. Luckily, those were tight at the ankles and wrists. This outing, usually fifteen minutes, took me close to three hours.

Doris and Eric were baptized together later in spring. Coming home from the Lutheran Church at Academy and Wellington, I was a tired, worn-out mother, holding the baby in my right arm, Doris holding tightly onto my left hand. Looking pretty, Bella walked on my right. Daddy was a few steps ahead of us taking photographs.

FLIGHT INTO THE UNKNOWN

At Easter, we took a walk in Assiniboine Park. Even with a little snow still on the ground, we threw colourfully wrapped Easter eggs ahead when the girls were not looking. We pointed them out, and the kids had fun running to pick them up. They believed the Easter Bunny had dropped them. On my arm, Eric bundled up in his light-blue snowsuit felt heavy, but I could not bear handing him to my husband. We still had no stroller, and he had outgrown Doris' doll pram.

Louis' youngest sister, Barbara, visited us during the summer. The weather was dry and sunny; we enjoyed beautiful walks in Winnipeg's different parks. I gave her a facial one afternoon using my expertise in aesthetics. She talked about my wedding, apologized for not having attended but asked me,

"Do you have any idea who sent you the black-rimmed telegram with condolences for your wedding?"

"What? I have never seen a telegram like that."

First, a hot, then a cold shiver went up and down my back. That could only have been my abuser and stalker in Germany, the one who had said, "If I can't have you, nobody will. I'll shoot first you and then myself if you ever have a boyfriend." He had held a pistol to my head once before. He had found me after I had escaped at Christmas 1956, hiding with friends. He was a married man in power. I couldn't report him; nobody would have believed me, the 'Ossie,' the second-class citizen. Initially, he had been the reason I had wanted to leave Germany to be free.

My sister-in-law noticed my hands were shaking.

"Giselle, you know who could have done that? If you never saw the telegram, then Mui must have kept it hidden from you in order not to ruin your day. Do you want to talk about it?"

"No, Barbara, I don't. Maybe I should be glad that Mui kept it from me. It upsets me even now. All I can tell you, it must have been a man who had power over me, and I did not want him."

By now, Louis had five employees. During my pregnancy, I had met an older woman who became my best friend, Marianne Ewy. She would occasionally look after my girls. I could drop them off at her place, or I could pick her up and take her to our home. Marianne lived close to our business. She had a beautiful cat, and the girls loved being there, playing with it. I tried not to take advantage. I was still chauffeuring everyone multiple times a day, Louis to work, girls to school, and coming home before the girls. I was late once, and they stood in front of the door, hugging each other for warmth. I felt very guilty. From then on, Bella had a string with a house key around her neck. They often spent time at the office. Both liked to draw; it kept them occupied.

Life was busy. One of the German Consular ladies' group recommended a seamstress. She made a dress for me out of a piece of silk I had brought with me from Germany. In exchange, I did a facial and pedicure for her. She had two children. She offered to sell me her stroller for $25.00 and laughingly suggested,

"Promise to sell it back to me if I get pregnant again." Which happened a year later.

I remember a day in our backyard. The girls were sitting on a blanket playing with their dolls. Bundled up, baby Eric had a horrible cold and was lying in the stroller next to them. He looked quite sick. I was afraid he might die. It made me feel anxious and nervous. I was jumpy, kept running up and down to the basement to do the laundry with that wringer washer. I was thankful we had a clothesline outside, and I could keep an eye on Eric while hanging my washing. Luckily, he recovered within two weeks.

Christmas 1966 was different. At dusk on Christmas Eve, we attended the German service at St. Peter's Evangelical Church on Wolseley, met and greeted our new German friends. After the service, we drove along prestigious Wellington Crescent to look at the Christmas decorations on the large riverside houses. After coming back to our small cozy home, we enjoyed previously prepared traditional potato salad with European wieners. The natural Christmas tree looked great, lit with two sets of twelve electric but real-looking white candles, made in Germany. The girls couldn't wait to open their presents. There were parcels from my parents, Louis' parents, his birth mother Granny, Doris's Aunt Anna, the parents of their biological mother, and, naturally, from us. Nothing from Kirsten. Not even a card. We were careful never to mention her in front of the children. Bella couldn't remember her anyway, and Doris, who had met her in Toronto, never asked.

FLIGHT INTO THE UNKNOWN

12: ADENAUER - A CELEBRATION OF LIFE

Conrad Adenauer was the mayor of Cologne until he got the order to form a new federal government in 1949, combining the three western sectors of Germany, governed by the American, British and French occupational forces. Instead of neutrality, Adenauer chose to work closely with the allied powers. On May 23, serving from 1949-1963, Adenauer became the first Chancellor of the new country officially called the Federal Republic of Germany - known in the English-speaking world as West Germany. He created the so-called 'Wirtschaftswunder,' the economic miracle, placing this new state in third place in the world for its high living standard, unbelievable after the total devastation of WWII. Inflation stalled with the introduction of new money, people worked hard for long hours, and foreign guest workers arrived due to the shortage of men. Adenauer secured NATO membership, made relevant trade agreements, and was revered both by the Germans and the Allied forces, who kept a strong presence in the country.

Following the formation of the Bundesrepublik in the west, the Soviet Union, the occupying force in the east, followed suit. They formed the Deutsche Demokratische Republik, known as DDR or East Germany. They also printed new money. Each person received 20 of the new Marks; since there were six people in our family, we received 120 Marks. Many people escaped to West Germany. Life in the two Germanys couldn't have been more different: It was like 'The Prince and the Pauper.' In the passing years, economically, it slowly got better in the east, but political oppression got worse. When I escaped in 1955, the fleeing numbered in the thousands each day. Within five years, they built the infamous Berlin Wall, securing the borders with death strips and barbed wire to keep the people in instead of invaders out.

The catalyst for all the changes had been Conrad Adenauer, who gave work and life back to the Germans in the west, much admired internationally. He died on April 19, 1967.

At that time, we were actively participating in the vibrant cultural life in Winnipeg: the German Club, the German Canadian Business Association, and the Consular Diplomatic Corps. Balls, receptions, house parties and even ladies' coffee and chat afternoons were part of it. We received an invitation for an exclusive Celebration of Life for the great German Chancellor, organized by the German Consulate. The American and other international consuls and diplomats, as well as the Manitoba Premier and his entourage, the mayor of Winnipeg and political party leaders, made up the several hundred people invited to attend. The embossed invitation requested formal wear, black suits for men, dark suits, gowns or cocktail dress, and hats worn by the ladies.

My husband still had his 'multiple wedding suit.' When he dressed on the big day, his pants had 'shrunk' about six inches from hanging in the closet. What to do? We only had an hour to get ready. I took the seam in the back apart, attached a piece of elastic to both sides and - voilà, he could close the pants in the front. If he didn't button it, the jacket still fit. It had a slit in the back, and when he moved his arms up to straighten his tie, his white shirt would show half-way down his backside. I warned him not to raise his arms, be careful when hugging people and remain aware of the embarrassment he could face. I started giggling even before we left. He chimed in and mentioned how good it was we did not have to use the 'Thousand Year Reich Salute' anymore.

"That would be my undoing!"

Since I did not own a black hat, I went to Eaton's and found a lovely looking one, a shiny plastic weave. I was upset about the high price of 24.00 dollars, enough to buy twenty-five pounds of ground beef. But I needed a black hat. I carefully removed the price tag at home. I felt silly but elegant wearing it. Seeing my women friends, I thought I looked better than some of them did

FLIGHT INTO THE UNKNOWN

with obviously more expensive hats. Several ladies even complimented me, asking where I had found such an exquisite hat. I still had that giddy feeling about my husband's pants, and I kept an eye on him. Observing the politicians with their sombre expressions put a different twist on the whole affair. When the German consul's wife, a good friend, hugged Louis, the back of his jacket opened up, and a lady next to me opened her mouth and stared. I tried hard not to laugh, touched her arm and told her what I had done with his pants. She was worse than me, could hardly contain herself and held her handkerchief in front of her face. Several other ladies had seen it too. In no time, five or six of us tried to keep sombre faces. I moved to stand behind Louis.

Poor Conrad Adenauer! As a born Rhinelander, he unquestionably would have enjoyed it. Before he became the great Chancellor, he had delivered many Carnival speeches in Cologne. Despite the sombre affair with all the political statements, for us, it surely was a Celebration of Life. Very uplifting! Louis and I avoided looking at each other to control our funny bone.

The next day, with the price tag re-attached to my hat, I went back to Eaton's. Louis exclaimed, "You can't do that!"

He couldn't stop me. The sales lady asked me why I wanted my money back.

"My husband doesn't like it. Typical man. You know how they are."

"Do you want to exchange it for another? Or you could buy something else…"

"Really? He will tease me if I come home with another hat. I'll be a nice mommy and buy something for the kids."

With little Eric on my hand, we went up an escalator. Coming back down, I lifted the boy with his hand in mine over the edge to step off. A gentleman behind me did not smile when he said,

"Don't worry if you pull his arm off. He still has another one."

I bought two pairs of shorts and two pretty T-shirts for the girls and still received a bit of change. I graciously put it in the can for the Red Cross next to the cash register.

My husband's multiple wedding suit became the 'Adenauer Memorial Suit.'

FLIGHT INTO THE UNKNOWN

13: MEMORY OVERLOAD

We had sent lots of photographs to my parents over the years. Listening to all the speeches at the Adenauer Celebration of Life, my family's letters had unleashed a great deal of longing in me. They were getting on, and I felt the need to see them again. I wanted my son to meet his grandparents and his great-grandmother before it was too late. My life had been a roller-coaster with little time to think much of my past. I conjured up memories, too many memories. My family lived on the shore of the Baltic Sea, and I remembered many experiences at the beach back home. The years at the Kanu Club, my boat Max, which my dad had to sell after I escaped East Germany, my kayak races, my old friends - I had a bad case of memory overload.

It was a foolish thing to follow my heart, but I asked my parents in East Germany to apply for a visa for me to visit. To our surprise, permission was granted. My escape in 1955 was a criminal act punishable with a 30-year prison sentence and nothing but bread and water. Now, twelve years later, and with an official visa, I believed the authorities had forgiven me. I was anxious, but I wanted to see my family so very badly. I hoped it was safe with my landed immigrant status in Canada noted in my passport, with a Canadian husband, children, and my married name.

Eric was born in Canada and was a Canadian citizen by birth. I had a West German Passport. My child was listed in my husband's Canadian passport, not in mine. All I had was a note stating I was allowed to take his son to Germany with me.

GISELLE ROEDER

I was born in Pomerania and had lost my roots when my homeland was ceded to Poland after WWII. I spent my teen years in East Germany. We were refugees, evicted from our home. The people around us never accepted us. I escaped to West Germany and there too, I was considered a second-class citizen, the 'Ossie.' Did I have roots? No, they were destroyed. Did I have feelings of belonging? No, they did not exist. I was a leaf blowing in the wind. My baby boy, born in 1965, welded our family together, my husband and the two stepchildren. Without Eric, I might have left Canada and gone back to Germany.

With my baby in my lap, I flew from Winnipeg via London to Frankfurt, where my in-laws picked us up. We had a wonderful week with them. They spoiled their new grandson. After that, we boarded a train in Wiesbaden, and at the border crossing in Lübeck, the guards stamped my entry into East Germany, no questions asked. To meet my parents was almost traumatic. They were shaking; tears were running out of my dad's eyes, my grandmother cried as she held her first great-grandson, the first male baby born into our family since 1909. I remember Eric playing with her earlobes when looking into her eyes. We came in time because, sadly, Grandmother died six weeks later. On this sunny afternoon at the end of May 1967, we looked at one another, not quite knowing what to say. It was hard to believe that after so many years, separated by the Berlin Wall and the fortifications between East and West Germany, we could touch each other, smile at each other, and hug each other.

At 7:30 in the morning, I took the train to the city of Bergen on the island of Rügen. We had to register our arrival at Police Headquarters and receive our departure permission stamp for a week later. Little did I realize the trauma awaiting us. They took my passport. They held me and my toddler captive because he had no passport. My husband's note, allowing me to take his son to Germany, was useless. They threatened to keep my baby because he had no passport. We did not know a baby needed a passport! They told me a child is a non-person without a passport. They claimed to have every right to take him away from me, and he would belong to the State: The State of East Germany, that is.

Oh, my God!

FLIGHT INTO THE UNKNOWN

Different officers interviewed me at intervals throughout the day. We had no food, no drink. They allowed me to go into town around noon to buy some food because, without a passport, I could hardly run away. All I could find was some fake chocolate called Vitalade. I had no clean diapers for the baby, and I could not buy any. We had anticipated returning on the next train before 10:00 AM. My little one-and-a-half-year-old boy charmed the officers and many people waiting with us, sitting on long hard flat wooden benches in the front hall. Every face showed the strain of hiding the fear of what might happen next. Nobody felt secure, and everybody was too scared to talk. Too often, people just disappeared and were never seen again.

Little Eric walked around on his short legs, stopping and smiling, wanting to give hi-fives, which nobody understood until I explained, and he said 'Hi' to everyone. He was like a ray of sunshine in the old decrepit building; he lit up the grey walls, which felt as if they were closing in on us. I was amazed my child was such a good boy. You could feel the tension in the air, and the few other children present pressed close to their mothers or fathers. I am sure, because of my happy boy, all the people waiting forgot their worries for a few moments as they watched the unafraid small Canadian kid.

The police had a box of index cards in the interview room with everything noted: My education, my achievements in kayak sports, family members, and even uncles and aunts in east or west, cousins and close friends, my work-related activities and my escape. They had it all in front of them. I answered all their questions truthfully as I realized they knew all the answers anyway. One of the officers dwelled on my escape and mentioned it was still considered a criminal act. I tried to explain it with my youth at the time, it had a lot to do with a boyfriend, and having been blinded by stories about the west. I just did not know better and had to learn some hard lessons because of it. One thing they didn't know about was how the headmaster of the school where I was teaching had attempted to blackmail me. He promised to protect my parents and me from political oppression if I slept with him. This man knew that my father, after two years of hard labour in Siberia, was not a communist. He also knew that my parents were the reason I had not joined the political party as was required for all teachers. I had not reported him since that would have landed all of us in prison. Except for my father, I never talked about it; it was the real reason for my escape. My father had said to me, 'Hau ab,' meaning 'get lost' when I had told him about it. I did not even say goodbye to my mother that last evening to protect her during interrogations by the police after my sudden disappearance. She could not lie, and what she didn't know - she couldn't tell.

One of the interviewers asked a lot of questions about Canada. He wanted to know how difficult it was to emigrate and how life was in Canada compared to Germany, East or West. I tried to explain it was just like everywhere else. The people have to work hard, and the Canadians also just cook with water. I talked about my two stepchildren and how disappointed they were that they couldn't come. I had promised they could accompany me next time, implying I wanted to visit again. I mentioned that my husband was even afraid I might choose to stay in Germany. The officer took a lot of notes. I felt sure he asked more than he was required to ask officially. I tried to gain his sympathy. I smiled and implored him to speed up the process of my entry and exit stamps because of Eric's smelly diaper.

I had to remove his poop with pieces of newspaper in their toilet but could not change him. After my interrogations, I waited for nearly another four hours. By this time, it was close to 6:00 PM, no more customers waiting, and many officers leaving. I was afraid they would lock me up for the night, so I stopped one and insisted that I speak to the head of the police station. Finally, I was admitted to the Police Chief's office. My baby was wet, dirty and hungry and not so happy anymore. I commented that my husband would surely get the Canadian Government involved, and I needed his permission stamp for my baby and me to leave and go back to Canada.

With a little smile, he listened to me, opened his drawer, extracted my passport, leafed through it, then pushed it over the desk and said,

"Enjoy your stay in our Democratic Republic and have a good trip home."

Next to the departure stamp was already noted: 'Permission to leave for Canada with a child born on November 19, 1965.'

FLIGHT INTO THE UNKNOWN

Stunned, I stared at him. He laughed; for him, it was a joke, the highlight of his day.

Arriving back in Canada, I wanted to kiss the ground. I experienced a definite sense of belonging, the feeling of coming home. I looked up to the vast blue prairie sky with a silent prayer of thanks. Within days I filled out the application to become a Canadian citizen and surrendered my West German citizenship. I have kept the invalidated German passport with those notes in it. It was one of my proudest moments when I stood with about twenty other people and took the oath to be of service to Canada and a loyal subject of her Majesty, the Queen.

"This Land is my Land…"

It is now more than fifty-six years since I first set foot on Canadian soil - but this is where I belong, belong with body, heart, and soul. One day, my ashes will be part of Canada, the land where I had unconsciously grown roots.

FLIGHT INTO THE UNKNOWN

14: 767 DORCHESTER AVENUE

One day in June, my neighbour from across the street called on me.

"Giselle, we are moving. Our house will be for rent. You told me you love it, so I'm telling you first. You need to phone Mr. Moffat if you want it."

"Oh, Anita, that is great news. Thank you so much." I hugged her and, laughing, we did a little dance on the sidewalk.

Louis agreed, and I was in seventh heaven when we got the go-ahead to move in as soon as the Thiessen family moved out. It gave me quite a lift. Here, I could create a beautiful home for us.

767 Dorchester was an old house with two full stories and a third with gable windows with finished attic rooms which, once upon a time, were the maid's quarters. Those rooms became the domain of my girls. This house, with its beautiful interior layout, was just one of a whole row of similar homes. All but ours were owner-occupied. Our house was white with green trim and had flower boxes under the many windows. I needed ninety-eight geraniums to fill the boxes every spring. It was a sight to behold. In the fall, I would plant a hundred pots with cuttings and grow them on the window sills indoors in preparation. Imagine how long it took each day to water all those plants. In summer, in full bloom, they made the house look luxurious.

A large screened porch covered the entrance area to protect against the plentiful Winnipeg mosquitos and doubled as a place to leave our shoes or boots. I added a sitting area and a coat rack. A bright hallway and a wide stairway leading to the second floor formed the heart of the old house. Through French doors on either side of the hall, one entered into a large dining room on the right and a charming living room with lots of windows and an open fireplace on the left. The built-in white breakfast nook with red trim in the kitchen was one of our favourite spots. It was the children's place to do their homework while I was preparing our meals. There was a sink in the middle of the long counter, plenty of cupboards and an old but working rounded fridge. I was thankful for the more modern stove.

Mr. Moffat came to collect the rent every month and occasionally stopped by to say hello and chat. I loved him, and he liked me too. The kids adored him; he was almost like a grandfather to them since they didn't have any other family in Winnipeg. We loved living in his old house. The two years we lived here were my happiest in good old Winterpeg. Mr. Moffat always complimented me on my hard work and transformation of the garden. Colourful summer flowers followed the spring flowers, and big sunflowers stood guard. The tomatoes, thriving along the sunny side of the single garage, still tasted as tomatoes should. In front of those, I planted chives, parsley, lettuce, and green onions.

I tried to copy Hertha, one of our German friends. Her garden was the most fantastic I had ever seen. She and her husband had a large river lot with plenty of old trees. When their daughter graduated, she went to Germany to study at the famous Heidelberg University. A few years later, she married her professor. Hertha was sad when her son also went back to Germany. Resigned to it, she said,

"We left Germany to give the kids a better life in Canada, and they go back to live where we came from."

Her garden was her solace, her pride and joy. She gave me a gorgeous 'Bearded Lily' and close to it sprouted a tiny oak tree from an acorn. I babied the tree. I even took it with me when we had to move again. I learned a lot from Hertha, and she gave me advice as well as new plants or seeds she had harvested.

My father was now over 65 years old, and East Germans of that age were able to get a visa to travel to the west for three weeks. If they didn't return, it would save paying them their old age pension. I sent a flight ticket for Dad to my sister Christel, and she took him to the passport office in Hamburg, where he received a West German passport. To fly to Canada was verboten to East Germans – he had to avoid getting any customs or entry stamps into Canada in his East German one. They kept it for him until he returned. I called my sister when he was with her, and he asked me:

"Gila, wouldn't it be better if I take the train to Frankfurt and start the flight there? If I fly from Hamburg to Frankfurt, I might not get a seat on the overseas' flight, and I'll have to stand all those hours to Winnipeg."

I laughed. "Dad, yes, you may have to hold onto straps like in an overcrowded bus! Don't worry; your seat is reserved."

With my father, I never knew when he was joking. It was heartwarming to have him, and the children were excited to show him everything. He gave me his passport for safe-keeping. When we took him for a walk along Wellington Crescent later that day, he asked for his passport. I asked him why he wanted it.

"What if the police stop us and I don't have it? At home, we even have to take it to the outhouse."

"Dad, you are in Canada, no police will stop you. Here you only need it to travel across borders."

On Wellington, he looked at all the big trees along the boulevard and whispered,

"Are there any wild Indians, will they shoot at us with arrows?"

Joking again. A few days later, we visited a unique shop - a taxidermist. Canadian taxidermy covered all the walls, from fish to fowl; there were bears and all other Canadian critters in another room. He was fascinated by a fish covered with rabbit fur. He looked at the proprietor and said in German,

"That is a funny-looking fish. Why does it have fur?"

To my surprise, the taxidermist answered in the same language. "Because it lived in icy waters close to the North Pole. It's cold there."

The facial expression of my dear old dad was priceless. I saw the wheels turning in his head, not sure to believe it until we all laughed. The whole time in Winnipeg, he was like a child in wonderland. He was amazed by the freedom we had in this incredible country. Just to show him what the US border was like, we crossed it close to Altona, Manitoba. A beam was across the road, a little shack on the right, no guard in sight. I called out, and, a few minutes later, an officer came around the shed, approaching us while buttoning his fly.

"Hello! All Canadians? Where are you headed?"

"We'd like to look at the sunflower fields a few miles from here. They are supposed to be fantastic. We'll be back in a couple of hours."

With that, he waved us off. "Okay, have a good day! See you later."

My father was skeptical. "Thaaat is the American border? I can't believe it! Too bad I can't talk about it when I come back home."

I was despondent when his time was up, and he had to leave. We both cried when hugging at the airport.

"Dad, as soon as Mom is old enough (women had to be 60), you'll both come, okay?" He was quite emotional but gave me a nod.

Louis had hired a receptionist, and I was no longer required to be in the office every day. I still did the books at home. A monthly coffee gettogether with about a dozen German women, held in our different homes, was a highlight of my social life. It was usually from 2.00 to 4.30 PM while the girls were in school. I became part of the group and happy to bring my toddler. I wasn't worried if I was a little late coming home because the backdoor was always unlocked. Nobody locked their doors in the sixties.

A week or two before the coffee afternoon at Hertha's house, little Eric had pushed a footstool next to our stove, climbed up, and switched on an element. Trying to get to the others, he had placed a hand on the hot one.

"Mommyyyyyy!" He was screaming like a pig about to be slaughtered.

With dirty hands, I came running from my garden. Eric's hand was burned but had healed somewhat when we went to visit Hertha. Once there, he went from one lady to the other, showing each one his wounds with a sombre expression and enjoyed the attention.

On one such afternoon, I met Gerti. She had three children; her youngest girl was the same age as Eric. Gerti offered to babysit

FLIGHT INTO THE UNKNOWN

Eric at her house when I had to work, and the two youngsters became partners in crime. I hoped they might marry later in life, but it did not happen. I still believed that it was okay for me to be naked around my baby, or even get into the bathtub together. Louis was against it. One evening, only wearing my pyjama bottoms, I was brushing my teeth, leaning over the sink. Eric came into the bathroom, stood beside me, chattering away about his day. After a moment of silence, he asked me,

"Mommy, why are your boobs so round?"

I almost swallowed my toothbrush. I kept brushing and mumbled,

"Why do you ask?"

"Mrs. Gerti's are long."

Leaning even lower over the sink, I asked,

"Which do you like better?"

"The long ones…"

What? Not even three years old, and he has an opinion about breasts? I was disappointed he didn't choose mine but explained,

"Women are like flowers. God made many different ones; that's why. But how would you know?"

"Oh, Lori and I went into the bathroom, and her mom was in the bathtub. I saw it."

Well, that was it. Eric never had a bath with me or saw his mommy in the nude again. For once, I admitted his father had been right.

Christmas, the first year in the old house, was an exceptional occasion. We covered the French glass doors with packing paper to give Santa privacy to bring his presents. We had a seven-foot Christmas tree decorated with the 24 German-made white electric candles, apple-sized blue ornaments, and lots of silver tinsel. It looked incredibly elegant. We added home-baked Christmas cookies and chocolate pretzels. I wanted to create a Christmas tradition, so I used the same decorations for many years despite the children's wishes to have colourful lights like their Canadian friends. The cookies and chocolate pretzels, hanging within reach, were devoured within days.

We often observed the kids lying on the floor looking under the locked doors. They could not see anything since a thick rug obstructed the view towards the tree. Even the small cat we adopted would lie there with them. It was a funny little kitten, it made us laugh, and all of us loved it.

Thick snow covered the ground when we drove to the German Christmas Eve service at St. Peters. The kids couldn't sit still during the sermon but were fascinated by the children acting out the Nativity scene with Mary and Joseph and the baby Jesus. It even was a real baby. The church felt festive illuminated with many candles, a huge decorated Christmas tree, and a choir singing lovely German Christmas songs. It was beautiful and, for me, emotional. Once again, we drove along Wellington Crescent after the service to see the famous Christmas decorations on the million-dollar-homes - but our dear children were restless and kept asking to go home.

"We saw all these houses last year! Why do we have to do it again? Let's go home to see our own Christmas tree."

We did not relent; we pointed out several huge smiling snowmen, some moving and waving, Santa with sleigh and reindeer on roofs, and some incredible homes decorated with thousands of lights. Dad drove slowly, then took his time to park the car in the garage. The entrance was off the back lane, getting into it wasn't easy because of all the snowbanks. Finally, the kids were allowed to get out of the car. All three ran to the house, and one of the girls yelled,

"The Christmas tree lights are on! Santa was here! Mommy, Daddy, hurry up, let's get inside…"

They couldn't wriggle out of their snowsuits and boots fast enough. I had the dinner table set in our nook. Like every year, it was potato salad and sausages, my Christmas tradition. I sent the kids to the bathroom to wash their hands.

When they returned, Dad had removed the paper from the doors, and they could see the festive living room, but the doors were still locked. Nerve-racking for the children, having to eat dinner first. They weren't even hungry anymore.

At last, we entered the room. Each of the children had learned a little poem weeks before Christmas. Now they had to recite them to the non-present Santa. We would sing 'Oh Christmas tree, oh Christmas tree,' and only after all that could they dive in and find presents with their names on them. I told them,

FLIGHT INTO THE UNKNOWN

"If you undo the ribbons without breaking them or ripping the paper, you can make a wish!"

My parents had taught me that. Because of the war, we couldn't buy anything new. We had to save ribbons and paper if we wanted anything other than newspapers to wrap presents. Within minutes, the living room looked like a disaster area. It was a prosperous Christmas with many gifts from the three sets of grandparents, three aunts, and us. Eric received a little green Volkswagen pedal-car, he could sit in it and steer but had to pedal to move it. He was in seventh heaven and declared,

"I will race along the sidewalk after the snow is gone!"

He did, hard to believe that he could pedal so fast. We had a cozy evening. Daddy had a beer, and Eric had his first sip, asked for another and became a little tipsy. Dad put a bit of beer on the cat's plate, she licked it up, and I don't know which was funnier: Eric dancing like 'Frosty the Snowman' or the cat, unsteady on its feet and playing with the colourful piles of paper. We laughed more that evening than we had for months.

FLIGHT INTO THE UNKNOWN

15: NEW CHALLENGES

The year 1968 came with a lot of work. What else is new? Louis grumbled that Aetna Photo was getting too busy, and he must soon look for larger premises. I dreaded it.

I had saved $300 commission from my German movie paper. I bought a used blue Volkswagen Beetle. It had been a smoker's car and stunk to high heaven, but it was in good driving condition. I used all kinds of cleansers and sanitizers, but they didn't do the trick. The children helped and were excited that we had our own car. I bought new seat covers. It was time I became independent, having to drive to the different German shops for ads, often with three children in tow. I also gave more and more lectures for women's groups, even to entertain women at Conventions while their husbands were busy with seminars. I was slowly making a name for myself as a speaker. My idea about 'Skincare from the Inside Out' was new in Canada.

Louis' oldest sister, Marion, came to visit. She was a great knitter; her hands were always moving. She didn't even look at the design she was creating. She brought a smart sleeveless dress for me and one for each of the girls. They were always dressed like little princesses. I thought of them that way with their aristocratic background. They were pretty, and I was proud of them. Bella had blond curls and blue eyes with a likeness of her father; Doris had chestnut-red straight hair and brown eyes. My friends always commented,

"Bella looks like her dad, but Doris gets her looks from you."

Not even our closest friends knew that I was not their birth mother.

I took Marion on a sightseeing tour of Winnipeg. We were back home at four o'clock. Louis came home early, and I was wondering why the girls weren't home yet at 4:30. When the phone rang, Louis answered it.

"I am the manager of the Payfair convenience store. You better come to pick up your daughters. They are in my office. We will not release them until you are here."

Marion stayed with Eric. Louis and I went to get the girls, wondering why they held them. We were shocked to learn they had helped themselves to large chocolate covered marshmallows. A store clerk had noticed Doris with one hand under her dress, and when asked what she was doing, she cried out,

"I can't find my sister; I can't find my sister..."

They found Bella close to the second exit. She could have left but was afraid to go without Doris. She had also hidden marshmallows under her skirt. They had no money to pay for them. Louis could hardly contain himself; without the manager present, he might have lost it as he had quite a temper and a quick hand. We paid for the stolen goods and bought more of the same for $13. It exceeded my budget for the week. For $9.98, I could buy ten pounds of ground beef. At home, in Marion's presence, Louis faced the girls, gave them a lecture about stealing, and declared:

"You will eat marshmallows for breakfast, lunch, and dinner until they make you sick."

There was no reaction. I don't remember what kind of dinner we had. Marion helped me cook, and she was good at it. The girls munched their marshmallows, the same followed for another two days, breakfast, lunch, and dinner. They never complained. By the third day, I could not stand it anymore. My health-conscious mind prompted me to fight with their dad in our bedroom.

"They need protein; they need a fresh salad; we can't keep this up, just letting them eat sugar..."

Louis kept calm.

"During the war, you and I had less to eat. We had to eat turnips instead of marshmallows. We are alive and healthy. They are not starving."

FLIGHT INTO THE UNKNOWN

We had quite an argument; in the end, he gave in. It was Marion's last day, and we had barbequed chicken, rice, and veggies. I served the girls, and again, there was no reaction. After supper, a grinning Louis asked his daughters,

"So, what would you like for dessert?"

After a little pause, Doris answered for both of them.

"Marshmallows…"

I bit my lips and glanced at Marion, she burst out laughing, I followed suit, Louis looked surprised but joined in. So much for feeding them marshmallows until they got sick! Later, alone in our bedroom, he was mad at me. I had ruined his intentions; I should have left him to deal with his children; I should not interfere. He was furious with me. It wasn't the first time; it happened whenever I took the children's side. When Marion talked with the girls, Doris was telling her,

"We knew Mommy couldn't stand it for long. We already decided to ask for marshmallows as soon as we got a real meal again."

Wow, those little smarties. But I was more than disturbed and hurt when I started to notice money missing out of my wallet for several days in a row. I had never checked, I don't know how long this had gone on. I never believed my girls would do that, but it became apparent. My purse was always in the pantry. They took money to buy sweets. Until now, they had no allowance. Louis and I discussed the situation and decided to give them a small weekly sum.

One warm July Sunday, Mr. Moffat turned up and was greeted with welcoming smiles. He had asked for both of us to be at home. He seemed uneasy. I asked him what was wrong. He sat down for tea, and after a few minutes, he told us he was selling the house. He was giving us three months' notice to move. I completely broke down. I cried and begged him to sell the house to us. It was out of his hands. A lawyer had bought up all the homes around ours. Our house was the last one he purchased. Mr. Moffat explained:

"I have held on as long as I could. They plan to demolish the houses to make room for an apartment block."

"Demolished? This beautiful house, demolished? No!" What a shame. It was heartbreaking. I so loved the place and cried myself to sleep.

We went house shopping. We couldn't find anything suitable to rent and decided to buy a bungalow with a low down-payment from a builder in a new suburb called Southdale. Louis' lawyer contacted a lawyer in British Columbia to sell his building lot there. He received $1,600 for it; the lawyer charged us $600. Later, when I visited Vancouver and told friends who had sold lots there as well, I learned lots were selling for $37,000, long before we even sold. A Real Estate agent had bought up the lots and sold them to a developer to build a huge shopping center. We wondered who made all that money on us poor Manitobans, far enough away not to know any better. We had no recourse.

For our new house, we chose a design with four bedrooms. We were able to change the plan and had the smallest one added to the living room, which became L-shaped. It was our den; built-in bookshelves covered one whole wall. A working desk for me was under the window. A sideboard and a filing cabinet completed my little office. The house would be ready for move-in on October the first.

In early August, I switched cars with Louis. He suggested I drive to Vancouver with the children to visit our old friends. I chose to take the route through the Okanagan Valley with lovely lakes, and many beach-side motels. One sunny afternoon, driving along the winding road, the kids asked for a pee stop. I pulled into a small gravel road, sheltered by some trees on the left and a hill on the right. Eric sat on his potty while the girls went up the mountain slope to find privacy behind some bushes. I saw them climbing up higher and higher. I shouted for them to come down. I cleaned Eric's little bum when, moments later, Bella came flying down, sliding along the road like a rag doll, with bloody scraped arms and legs, full of small gravel and slivers. Her pleated light blue skirt and top were torn, but luckily she did not break any bones. She was white as a ghost but did not cry. I cleaned her up a bit, helped her back into the car. She just sat there, shaking, and stared at me, whispering,

"I couldn't stop. I ran…"

"Why? Why did you run down the mountain? You never do that because nobody would be able to stop!"

"Doris dared me. I didn't want to, but she kept daring me…"

"Would you jump off a bridge if she dared you?"

FLIGHT INTO THE UNKNOWN

By that time, Doris came into view. She did not run down the mountain; she was safe. She felt pretty bad and was unusually quiet when she sat down beside Bella. I drove like the devil the next 75 or 100 kilometres the winding #3 highway Princeton - Hope. We arrived at the Hope hospital after 8:00 PM. Bella held onto me, she was still shaking. I got her inside, and the night nurse was shocked when looking at her.

"No doctor here at this time. I will phone one after I settle this girl. She looks awful."

It did not take long. The doctor took one look, asked me if the children in the car outside were mine and if we had accommodation. He knew we were not locals because of the 'Friendly Manitoba' license plate. He asked the nurse to phone a motel to make sure we had a bed for the night. The doctor wheeled Bella away, the nurse told me to come back after we had dinner, and the children were in bed. Better yet, she would give me a call.

It was after 11:00 PM when I got the call. The doctor pointed at a handful of gravel and slivers on a side table.

"Took me hours to remove all that. I have never seen anything like it. At one point, the girl must have passed out, but she never cried. She is still in shock. I gave her something; she will sleep through the rest of the night."

With bandaged arms and legs, Bella walked to the car with the help of the nurse. She seemed all right the next morning. She was starving since she hadn't had anything to eat since lunch yesterday. We moved on and found another motel in Harrison Hotsprings on our way to Vancouver.

We spent almost a week with Louis' friends Gary and Helen; their children were the same age as mine. We loved their motorboat and the cottage on rocky Keats Island. It was quite an experience to camp out there. I feared one of my kids would slip down a cliff into the water and drown. Instead of the children, it was almost me. A small tree saved me. As a thank you, I found and planted another tree in the rocky ground. I admired it years later. It had grown up while I had grown older. People slipping could now grab its full branches and hold on for dear life.

It was a beautiful holiday. Since I loved driving, I saw no problem taking five days driving back to Winnipeg. The Rockies and the blue sky of the prairie, and the endless grey band of the highway relaxed me. It was freedom! When we were tired of singing or playing, 'I spy with my little eye...' my kiddies would sleep. Bella's wounds were healing well. The daily swim in the salty ocean water might have helped.

Louis was happy to see us back. He had found a more substantial location downtown for his photo lab and was already working on it. He had taken on a silent partner who had invested $50,000 in Aetna Photo. This gentleman had a successful painting business, and his employees did all the painting. Dad smiled:

"Hey! All of you! I need your help! There is much to do. You can do the cleaning, packing, and move all the smaller items."

Our days didn't have enough hours. Carpenters built darkrooms and walls. Louis planned to have two reception areas with separate entrances: one for professional photographers, another for amateurs. My desk would be on the amateur side, his office behind it. When customers entered, I would have to run back and forth between the two reception rooms. Louis had ordered an exceptional machine from Germany, and when I saw the invoice of $176,000, I nearly had a heart attack. He and his partner had taken a considerable bank loan. He explained it to me:

"I will be the only one in North America to be able to print enlargements up to sixteen feet. The new museum in Victoria has ordered dozens of large pictures and even more big slides. That machine will pay for itself within a couple of years..."

His words in God's ear. My days didn't have enough hours. Louis joked that everyone has 36 hours: the day has 24, and the night has 12. Isn't that enough for you? Did he think I was Superwoman?

True to the contract, our new house was move-in ready on October the first.

In September, the children had started school in the new neighbourhood. Driving the kids to school each morning, I loaded the car with stuff and brought more boxes in the afternoon when I returned to pick them up. Our friends Inge and Peter offered us their garage for storage. They had bought one of the new houses and already lived there. Only large pieces of furniture remained for the moving company. I had watched our new home grow every single day, from digging the basement right to the finish, our first own house, a white stucco bungalow with light grey and yellow trim. We planned to enclose the future patio area between the back door and the freestanding double garage with a fancy curved rock wall. I decided to create the garden and do the landscaping myself. The tiny oak tree from 767 Dorchester received a prominent spot, and Louis teased me about my 'little twig.'

Our last evening meal before moving day consisted of leftovers, but I had baked an apple pie for dessert. I left the cake in the oven with the oven door slightly open so that the heat could dissipate. Our back door was always unlocked for the children to play outside. A screen door kept the bugs out. My husband and I drove out to the new house with both cars loaded with boxes late in the afternoon. When we returned, I simply shut the oven door and started cooking.

We were sitting around the table in the nook and chatted excitedly about moving and sleeping here for the last time. I served dinner and switched the oven on to warm up the pie. Everyone loved hot apple pie with vanilla ice cream. At last, I could sit down and start eating myself.

I was restless and got up again. Louis was annoyed.

"Why don't you finally sit still and eat, you drive me nuts…"

I went to check the pie. I opened the oven door and stumbled back, shocked, and screamed! Our neighbour's cat jumped out of the hot oven and almost into my face. The cat ran like crazy for the back door, scratched at the screen, and meowed loudly. What if - oh my God!

The pie was half-eaten, and we threw the rest out. The cat survived; for us, at least we still had vanilla ice cream for dessert. I was in no condition to even eat my dinner. The episode had shaken me up. Badly.

FLIGHT INTO THE UNKNOWN

16: LIFE TURNS UPSIDE DOWN

Moving house and business took a lot of energy. We were exhausted by Christmas. The children started to question the existence of Santa because there was one at every shopping centre. Mrs. Poles, our neighbour across the street, told me her husband had a Santa costume. "Would he play Santa for us?" I asked her.

"Oh, I'm sure he would love to," she responded. So we had our little secret.

On Christmas Eve, the children and I made music: I played the accordion, Bella played the small organ, Doris a flute and Eric sang. The Christmas tree lights were on, Daddy and the cat sat on the sofa listening to us. All of a sudden, we heard the traditional 'hohoho' outside.

"Ho-ho-ho - Merry Christmas!"

Then all was quiet. We paused for a moment and then kept on with our music. After a short while, our doorbell rang. Doris ran to open the door, followed by Eric. There he was, a prominent Santa in his red outfit with a long white beard, a bell in his right hand, and a sack over his left shoulder. Dad, Bella, and I peeked around the corner into the hallway. Bella grabbed my hand, Doris turned snow-white, Eric ran like the devil was after him and hid under his bed. I was afraid Doris would faint, so I jumped to hold on to her.

Santa was taking it all in and started to talk calmly to the girls. His reindeer were waiting for him just down the road. Dad went to find Eric to bring him back. Each child recited a poem. Santa reached into his sack and handed out presents. With loud bell-ringing and more 'hohoho,' he left us. Eric received a cloth teepee tent from his grandparents; he built it up and never came out of it the whole evening. When I got up the next morning to make breakfast, he was already inside it again, snuggled up with Minka, our cat.

No rest for the wicked. I tried to catch up on the bookkeeping. The week went fast. New Years' night, when everyone was sleeping, I sat in the dining room, rattling away on the old adding machine, trying to balance the books. To be out six cents bothered me. The garbage can next to me was almost full of adding paper, and Minka buried herself in it.

She was a curious cat and even trainable. We had a large white Chinese rug in the living room, and she learned to walk around it on the hardwood floor to be with us in the sitting corner. One night the kids had a bubble-bath, and all three were in the tub. The foam was up to the rim. Minka, sitting at the edge, tried to paw the foam. She slipped into the water, and before we knew it jumped out and escaped to the kitchen, hid under the table licking herself. It was a shock to see that a wet young cat was as skinny as a rat.

Louis traded in the old Ford Falcon for a used Dodge Charger. I worked full time again. It was no problem to get the girls to school, just across an empty lot. Eric came with me. On an icy cold winter morning, Louis' Charger got stuck in the freshly fallen deep snow when he was backing out of the garage. He took my old VW Beetle and made it to work and back. I shovelled the white stuff - but did not dare to use his car. It was not reliable in snow. I had to go shopping the next day, bundled up my son and, only two miles down the highway, the engine of my Beetle sputtered, and we rolled to a stop. I tried to restart - and saw the tank was empty. I bent over to switch to reserve. Also empty! It was thirty-eight degrees below zero, more than a mile to the shopping centre and even farther to the next gas station. I had no choice. I carried my toddler in his bulky snowsuit. With icycles on our lashes and red noses, we walked into Safeway. I collapsed onto the nearest bench, shaking with cold. The staff brought me some hot tea and warm milk for Eric. They called the Manitoba Automobile Association. My Beetle was rescued with a gallon of gas and brought to us. Dear Daddy was very sorry he had forgotten to tell me he switched

FLIGHT INTO THE UNKNOWN

to reserve the day before, and my feelings for him were as cold as we had been, walking the highway.

With the winter 1968/69 finally behind us, spring was in the air. I immersed myself in gardening and landscaping around the house. My girls helped me to lay down sod on Victoria Day. It was hot; sweat rolled down my neck. I wore only a bathing suit and no sunscreen on my back. I sat down on the backdoor steps in the shade to take a breather. Eric came out of the house,

"Oh boy, Mommy, is your back ever red! You're burned…" The sun had got me. I developed huge blisters, the worst sunburn of my life. Louis had to spread creamed cottage cheese on my back, as the doctor had advised. I had to sleep on my tummy for two weeks. I couldn't wear anything touching my skin and couldn't go anywhere.

On a sunny Sunday, we drove to a forest and dug out three small trees. Doris made a poem about 'The little Tannenbaum.' I planted them together on the corner of our lot. One was about three feet tall, the next was two feet, and the one Doris liked, was one foot. We had a triangular flower bed with my 'Oak Twig' in the middle. On our corner lot, I also planted a tiny weeping willow (it had cost 99 cents), and it grew up to become gorgeous. The last time I saw my 'Oak Twig,' it was about fifteen feet tall but very slim. It was a lone oak, and no other such tree was in the area. We completed the fancy curved stone wall and had a lovely airy but protected patio between the house and the garage. I topped each of the four pillars with a flowering basket. On the south side of the house, I created a flower bed with bulbs and alpine plants like Enzian and even Edelweiss. Along the neighbour's fence, I planted my favourite fruit bushes: several red and white currant. These weren't so lucky, creepy crawlers and other bugs ate the leaves, the birds harvested the berries before I could, and the bushes died.

As always, the year went on with lots of work, the business made a good start, and Louis hired more people. Elena, a pretty girl from Czechoslovakia and Wolfgang, a young German fellow, started an affair; they got married later. The premises had two washrooms, one for men and one for women. I didn't like cleaning them, but it became my job on Sundays when nobody saw me. I wanted to save money by not hiring a cleaner. It embarrassed me, and I never told anyone.

GISELLE ROEDER

By May 1970, we had twelve employees. Towards the end of that month, Canada Post went on strike. How would we ship the finished photography orders? I brought the Canadian orders to the Greyhound bus terminal and the ones going to the USA to the various Airlines.

Louis broke his wrist at the beginning of June. He hired a manager, gave him carte blanche to run the business, and flew to Germany for two weeks. I could not stop Don from causing more expenses. I found our embossed stationery outside next to the garbage bin. He had ordered new ones. I tried to prevent him from wasting our money, but he brushed me aside:

"I am giving Aetna Photo a new, updated look. Louis gave me his permission. I am the manager. You have nothing to do with it."

It was useless to argue with him. Paul, our silent partner, did not want to interfere. Since I was not involved in the business other than being an overworked, unpaid volunteer/employee, there was nothing I could do. I saved the stationery from the weather and took the boxes home.

The postal strike continued for six weeks. No mail orders arrived. Local ones did not bring in enough to pay the twelve employees, rent, taxes, and, of course, the unnecessary new manager. I could have done a better job running our business and saved us a lot of money. When Louis came back, he got an earful from me, but I couldn't get him to fire Don. In August, he talked with his partner, and they declared bankruptcy.

It was the last straw for me. I had a breakdown, was sick in bed for weeks. I did not want to see anyone; I did not want to speak or listen to anyone. I lost my drive for life. I felt embarrassed and ashamed that the business partner lost his investment. How could we face Paul and his wife in social settings? I did not want to show my face at the ladies' coffee afternoon or go to an evening party with our German friends. I brooded about how I could have saved the business. The bankruptcy, in my eyes, had been unnecessary, Louis trip at such a time, the useless new manager, the waste and changes he ordered - and how I could not stop the looming disaster. Since Aetna Photo was a limited company, at least we did not lose our house. But I had to sell my accordion as we had no money to buy groceries.

FLIGHT INTO THE UNKNOWN

One evening after dinner, I walked to the artificial lake in our neighbourhood. I wanted to drown myself. I thought of the children, especially of my little son. How could I do that to him? To remember his beloved mommy killing herself? Then it hit me: I can swim. Cold and depressed, I went home around 11:00 PM. I hoped Louis would be sleeping, but he sat in the dark kitchen.

"Where were you?" A quiet question with an underlying angry tone.

"I was at the lake."

"I was afraid you might be up to no good. How could you even think of it? If you did that to the girls, you'd ruin them for life. Their first mother ran away, and if you left them too, especially like that, they would never recover."

He knew I had been suicidal since the bankruptcy. His comment felt like blackmail, but I knew he was right. He never mentioned Eric. I felt like a bird in an open cage, but I was too scared or feeling too guilty to fly away. It was tough.

Louis was not just a knowledgable photofinisher but also a first-class photographer. While we were in business, he won almost every photo competition he entered. Some of his professional customers complained, implying the photofinishing of his photos was better than theirs. He stopped participating in contests. After we lost the business, he was lucky to get a position as the manager of the professional division of Winnipeg Photo Ltd. Winnipeg Photo was the largest photofinishing lab in Winnipeg. Most of our customers followed him. Life for Louis was now comfortable. He had never had an eight-hour, five-day a week job since we left Vancouver.

During the new school year, I taught a few gymnastic classes in our children's school. It was an extra-curricular activity; parents had to pay for their children to be involved, and I earned $3.50 an hour. I knew of a young girl, an Olympian, who lived in Winnipeg, her parents, both gymnasts, had converted their barn into a gym. It was the only other place where kids could get training in this sport. They were Germans, and their barn was equipped with everything needed to train new Olympians. I hooked up with them and referred several children from my classes. Several of the kids I taught made fun of the exercises. Their parents dropped them off at the school because it was cheaper than paying a babysitter.

One day, Minka fought with our neighbour's Siamese cat. Minka's injury festered and did not heal. Louis wanted me to put her in a bag with a rock and throw her into the river. He was against spending money on a veterinarian. Crying hard, I took Minka to the Humane Society, and I promised myself never to get another cat, love it and then lose it. The vet took Minka into another room. While waiting, I noticed a birdcage, housing a small blue-eyed kitten. This kitten talked to me with a complaining voice like a baby; it was heartbreaking. It went on until the vet returned, saying that Minka was at peace. She saw me looking at the birdcage. She told me this six-week-old male cat has all its shots, and it needs a home - wouldn't I take it? The blue eyes are from another race. I donated $5.00, took the little fury ball and put it in my Volkswagen. That small cat went crazy, racing around the car, into my hair, over my shoulders and almost caused me to have an accident. My kids were happy when I held it out to them:

"This is Max."

Max was funny. He followed the kids to school, waited at the door until someone opened it, slipped inside and always found Eric and sat beside him. It was a new open concept area school with just bookcases dividing the different classes. Eric had to bring Max home repeatedly. I tried to keep Max in the house, but after a couple of hours, he wanted out. He went back to school, always finding one of the kids.

We loved Max. He was the funniest cat I have ever known. He kept me company when I worked late. Like Minka, he loved the paper basket and either curled up in it or emptied it all over the floor. He unrolled the toilet paper and took it throughout the house. Max probably thought he was a kid. A few times, I saw him sitting on an old lady's lap in a rocking chair, out on the sunny porch at a neighbour's house. She was visiting from Edmonton. One day, Max was gone. We searched around the whole neighbourhood. Everyone helped to look for him for two days. We checked near every road, and we checked empty fields, we explored the shopping centre and even the Windsor Park area across the highway. We didn't find him or his body. One evening, standing around one of the artificial lakes, a lady said,

"You know what? I think the old lady from Edmonton must have taken him. Max disappeared when she left. "

FLIGHT INTO THE UNKNOWN

What? Would people do that? I wouldn't have thought of it, but it made a lot of sense. Finally, we called off the search. We never saw Max again.

Surprisingly, my friend Gela phoned and persuaded me to come to her coffee afternoon since we hadn't seen each other for a long time. They had a house with a pool, and I hadn't seen it yet. I went, and it was good to meet up with everyone. Nobody mentioned our bankruptcy. We were twelve, Gela had fancy cakes, and everybody was happy and exchanged the newest gossip. When I came home, Louis smiled; he was glad I had attended again. We chatted, and then he asked me,

"Who was there?"

I told him the names; we knew them all from previous winter parties. Without thinking, I added, "Oh yeah, there was one new lady. She is going to be your third wife."

As soon as I said this, I bit my lips. Where did that come from, I had never thought of it.

"What?! What did you say? Why would you say such a thing? Are you nuts?" He was quite agitated.

"Sorry, Louis, I don't know why I said that. I hadn't even thought about it. It just happened. It's a joke."

For him, it was no joke. I felt weird about it. I remembered my 19th birthday when my parents had emptied our bedroom for a party. I had invited my canoe club friends. We made pancakes, and once we were a bit tipsy, I started to read palms. The last one, my sister Ingrid, was only fifteen and asked, "Can you read mine too?" I did, and I blurted out, "well, for one thing, you won't live very long." She wanted to know if she would still get married.

My insensitivity shocked me, and I told her some white lies, not what I felt. It was supposed to be fun; I knew very little about reading palms. The experience was such I never wanted to look at anyone's hand again. After having her right arm amputated due to a sarcoma, Ingrid died only two years later. Even without palm-readings, I made a couple more such predictions without thinking. And now, had I predicted a third wife for Louis?

FLIGHT INTO THE UNKNOWN

17: COMIMG INTO MY OWN

Tired of suffering the winter blues, I changed Eric's room into a skincare studio. I painted the ceiling hot pink, papered the walls with a Victorian-style wallpaper, bought an old French Provincial glass-front cabinet and painted it white. I couldn't afford a professional treatment chair, but one of our two lawn chairs, covered with white sheets, served me well. I ordered my first shipment of creams and lotions from Dr. Grandel in Germany, and I was in business. All I had to do was talk about skincare, mention it in my monthly movie paper, and my first customers began booking appointments. I offered only European style facials. For each two hour facial, I charged $6.00. I booked only one customer for each evening after supper.

    I was now a stay-at-home mom and had time to look after my children. Dad left for work early. Eric moved into the girl's room; the girls got a large room in the basement and a bathroom with a shower. We had a place for a sauna. There was still room for a guest room and a rec room, planned for a later date. The basement had high ceilings, reasonably sized windows, and several electrical and water connections were roughed in.

    I became a regular contributor and was one of the first writers for the new 'alive' health magazine. Also, I got more involved with the German Newspaper. I started a column: "Fragen Sie Frau Gisela." (Ask Mrs. Gisela) A gentleman running a weekly German television show on cable TV asked for volunteers. I applied and was accepted. I attended one show; that was all the training I got. The production manager shocked me the following week.

"You'll have to do the show on your own. Mr. Schmidt won't be back. A letter found on his car last week, warned him to never show his face on TV again. They, whoever they are, threatened to blow up his car. He took it seriously. He won't admit it, but we think he knows who is behind it. Some old Nazi story."

"But – but - I have no idea what to do!"

"No problem. Here is a handful of letters. Read them, talk about them and answer where you can. If you can't, tell them you will check the topic, and you will do it next week. You can also talk about the shops you visit for your movie paper. You'll have to fill the hour."

The show was 'LIVE.' Despite being thrown into the deep end, it went quite well. I was afraid there might be a threatening note on my car, but Louis shrugged it off. He did have suggestions on how to make the show better. Renate Achenbach joined and became the 'News Reader.' I received material and videos with travel tips from Lufthansa and invited people from the German community for interviews. I showed hydrotherapy treatments. When I did an alternate foot bath with my two original German foot tubs, I pretended there was hot water in one and cold in the other. It was only cold water - coming from a garden hose connected into the studio. I explained how the procedure increased circulation and boost the immune system, even prevent the flu if done before it is fully developed. The telephone at the station started to ring and didn't stop.

People wanted to know if there was an English language version of it. The director asked me if I could do this, and I said yes. Following my program, many new cable connections were ordered. My English television show was born. I needed a title, and the first one I came up with was 'Giselle's Life Unlimited.' The title came to me in a dream. It gave me the chance to interview all kinds of people, writers, business people, travellers; you name it. It was unlimited. I never ran out of material. I did not get paid, and I did not mind. It was a lot of fun, I loved it, and I learned how to ham it up.

Various radio stations invited me to speak on talk shows. CBC Radio noticed me as well. They asked me to do a program at 6:30

FLIGHT INTO THE UNKNOWN

AM, answering health questions, right after 'This is Christine from the Toronto Stock Exchange.' I finished my part with 'This is Giselle Roeder in Winnipeg.' I had to join the Actor's Union and was paid $50.00 for each show. The female production manager of CBC TV was a business counsellor; we liked each other and kept in touch.

I used that sign-off on my TV show to create my brand. I met many interesting people. It would be too much to talk about all of them. I do have to share a few with you. Ingrid Rimland, a writer, impressed me. I read her book, 'The Wanderers', while cooking rouladen, a traditional German meal. Reading her story consumed me, and I forgot to watch the pot and did not notice the meat burning. The smoke was so thick that I had to open the windows. A neighbour must have called the fire department: a firetruck arrived. The only damage was the loss of my unique pot and the months-long smell of smoke in the house. Ingrid sold many books as a result of my passionate interview. Another program was great fun. A lawyer, who had agreed to be my guinea pig for a pedicure, exclaimed while we were on air:

"What? I have to take my socks off for a pedicure?"

Another show I did was about juicing. During those years in the seventies, you couldn't buy juicers in Canada. I had imported one from Switzerland. I was explaining the health benefits of fresh juice and started off making apple juice. Then I juiced both carrots and apples. Finally, I raved about the health benefits of red beet juice. I stuffed prepared pieces into the juicer but always looked at the camera, speaking to the people watching. My assistant Alice cried out,

"Giselle, stop! There is no glass under the spout!"

The blood-red juice ran over the side of the table, forming a puddle on the floor. Oh shit! The shout flew out of my mouth.

The next morning, a police officer rang my doorbell. I peeked through a side window as he stood in front of the door with shiny boots, pulling his belt into place. My mind went back to last night. I asked myself: Did I get caught speeding? I had a heavy foot, and I had two speeding tickets already. I smiled at him and asked what I could do for him.

"I saw your show last night. I want to know where I can buy a juicer like that?"

If I had been an enterprising person, I could have started a juicer business and made millions. Someone else did, but that is another story.

Eventually, doing both TV shows became a burden. Louis took over the German one, and he made a success of it, getting more volunteers involved. Occasionally, they needed me to be a guest or interviewer. Some business friends donated a portable video camera. Louis and his group went to events in the German Hall or other happenings. Some businesses were willing to make a nominal donation for the privilege of being profiled. They used the money to buy tapes and other items to improve their portable equipment. Once, I interviewed Ed Schreyer, the former Premier of Manitoba. Now he served as Canada's Ambassador to Australia.

In June 1972, 'alive' Magazine organized its first 'Health Retreat' at the Emerald Lake Chateau in Alberta. Part of my job, being one of the four keynote speakers, was leading the morning exercises. My other topics were hydrotherapy and living a healthy lifestyle. The publisher of the 'alive' Magazine, Siegfried G., was a vegetarian and oversaw the preparation of all meals. It was vegetarian food all week, except on Friday: fish day. Dr. Paavo Airola, one of the early alternative health advocates and Rebecca Clark, lectured on different topics. Rebecca had written a book about Devil's Claw root, 'How to Treat Arthritis.' I was in awe of her. Sadly, a couple of years later, she died of cancer.

Since the school holidays had started, I was permitted to bring my seven-year-old son, Eric. We had an entire guest cottage to ourselves. Siegfried's daughter, Eric's age, was also there. The two youngsters had lots of fun canoeing on the beautiful green Emerald Lake. Eric loved an outing with horseback riding. He looked as if he had grown up on a horse. My horse had a broad back, spreading my legs across it, hurt. Halfway up the mountainside, I got off and led it next to my son, who sat proudly in his saddle. Returning with the horse, the owner shook his head.

"That horse is way too big for you! Who the hell assigned it to you?"

After working for a year at the new company, Louis had a two-week vacation. He surprised me with tickets for a holiday in Tunisia. It was offered by a New York tour travel company for about $200.00 per person, including flights, hotels and two meals a

FLIGHT INTO THE UNKNOWN

day. We spent three nights in Copenhagen. We visited all the famous tourist spots, even a sex shop in the red light district. In one room, we could peek through tiny holes and see videos of different sexual acts performed. Seeing a man with a goat had me backing off in shock, and I ran for the exit. It was my only visit to a sex shop. I don't think I missed anything.

We landed in Tunis, Tunesia, on a bright sunny day. We loved our hotel on the beach. Dinner was never served before 9:00 PM, which made the days seem longer. We rented a tiny car. I drove. All of a sudden, we slowed almost to a stop, luckily we were going downhill. We pushed the car and were happy to see a gas station. They checked and told us in French there was no gas in it. What? A rental car is not filled with gasoline? There was only what the previous renters left.

We explored the countryside. A fascinating place was the camel market. We admired handwoven rugs, wondered why people on bicycles bought live chickens and goats. We learned people did not have fridges or ice boxes. I was intrigued by a mountain-high pile of buttons and asked how they got them. They had found every single one here or there. We came across a seller of camels, one of them was white. Louis asked,

"How much is the white camel?" The seller looked at me, then Louis, and answered,

"Two hundred-thirty-five Dinar, the same price as a good woman," pointing to me.

Young men had to pay for their brides with either several cows, a camel or other valuable possessions since they would take a worker away from their family. Most marriages were arranged at birth by the parents. Our taxi driver told us during our second week,

"It will take me four years to pay for my girl. We love each other, but I don't have anything to pay for her. So I save, and we wait."

For lunch, we chose a small native restaurant. We sat down at a small table, looked at the menu, but couldn't read it. The chef, who was also the server, waved us into the kitchen. He had at least six or eight pots going on a large stove. His cooking smelled good. He gave us a wooden spoon and indicated we should dip it into each one to find out what we would like to eat. He wasn't concerned about germs in the spicy food.

A round table was in the middle of the small restaurant. Several men came in, took their shoes off by the door and washed their hands in the sink we had overlooked when we entered. We felt embarrassed. The eight or nine men took seats around the big table. The chef put a bowl of something in the middle, gave each one a wooden spoon, and they all ate out of the one dish.

Later, we wandered along a lane with lots of artisans, making beautiful things out of brass, copper, silver, or wood. I admired a sizeable round brass plate. The base was brass, and the Koran was inlaid all around in small letters, one row with copper, the next with silver. We bought it. The young craftsman left his stall and accompanied us because he wanted to 'better his English.' He showed us where they, with the French army, had fought the Germans under Field Marshall Rommel.

"Oh, we loved Rommel. He was fair; he never shot a wounded man. All our girls wanted a Rommel baby, that's why you see many Tunisians with red or blond hair and blue eyes."

We looked at him, not quite believing, he became earnest and explained the German soldiers made the babies, not Rommel himself.

Darkness comes fast in Tunisia. We saw many walkers and joggers on the side of the road back to the hotel. People were coming home from work, and they were used to walking many miles every day. They lived in mud houses, palm or similar tree branches formed the roofs and slept on narrow beds made of the same material, a mud base, branches forming the mattress. We had visited one of those huts.

Back at the hotel, we were eight at our international round table. We needed to dress up for dinner. Women wore long gowns. Dinner was a three-course meal. The table setting was beautiful, soup plates for the first course set on a charger plate. We were the only ones going away exploring, so they listened attentively to our stories. I was excited to tell everyone about the brass plate we bought. A Danish woman, a fine china designer artist, asked,

"What is a plate?"

I grabbed the soup plate in front of me, tilted it up and explained,

FLIGHT INTO THE UNKNOWN

"THIS is a plate!"

The soup splattered all over the table. The soup was served. I had not noticed…

FLIGHT INTO THE UNKNOWN

18: MOSQUITOES, FISH AND A TAPEWORM

After returning from Tunisia, we had our first West German visitor in Winnipeg - my old kayak friend Klaus. It was exciting. He had brought a *Faltboot*, a portable two-seat kayak, packed into two knapsacks with two sets of paddles. What a great gift! He wanted to see more of northern Canada. We left Daddy to his own devices and drove to Lake Athapapuskow near Flin Flon. It was an 800-kilometre trip. We checked into a motel at the water's edge. A roadside statue of a funny cartoon character greeted us at the entrance to Flin Flon. There was a memorial next to it:

"Once upon a time, there was a mad scientist. His name was Josiah Flintabbatey Flonatin. He was the main character in a science fiction book the miners found in 1905 close to where they were working. Since the name was so difficult to pronounce, they shortened it to Flin Flon. As our village grew, it became our name in 1915."

It was much more fun to say 'Josiah Flintabbatey Flonatin' rather than Flin Flon. Every one of us repeated the name until we got it right, and trying it filled our car with laughter.

We cooked our meals outside on our camping stove. The motel provided fishing rods; Eric took one and was proud when he caught a small fish from the dock. He held it up and exclaimed,

"Can I eat this all by myself, Mom?"

Klaus caught a slightly bigger one. I cut it up and made rice with the fish pieces for the four of us. Eric's fish was steamed whole and served to him with rice. After dinner, I disagreed with

Klaus. He had refused to clean the fish and insisted it was a woman's job. Had he been teasing me, or did he mean it? It was hard to tell by his tone of voice or his facial expression. I was angry and upset when I pushed the kayak out onto the lake and paddled off into the sunset. I wore shorts and a sleeveless top and sat on my beach robe, planning to put it on when it cooled down. When miles out on the Athapapuskow Lake, I listened to the eery call of the loons and watched the sun drop below the horizon. It was time to turn around. The loons accompanied me but always dove and disappeared after a few seconds. Swarms of black mosquitos descended on me, and I couldn't get them off me by splashing wildly with the paddles, it was impossible. I couldn't take the time to put on my beach robe; I paddled like a madwoman. I was crying and ready to do what the loons did, dive under the water, but I was still far from the beach. It quickly got dark, and I wailed,

"Please, God, please help me! The mosquitos will kill me if I don't drown myself first."

It was an awful, terrible, even horrible experience. My crew was anxiously waiting for me. Eric almost cried when he said,

"Mom, you were just a dot on the lake, and then I couldn't see you anymore."

Klaus apologized profusely and promised,

"I won't fish anymore. Then we won't argue about the cleaning. I had no idea that you felt so strongly about it."

Mosquito bites covered every inch of my exposed skin. I developed an allergy; I now get huge bumps. The itch is so bad I want to scratch or cut them open.

The remaining bright sunny days made our life on the small sandy beach quite enjoyable. Klaus was a former East German Champion, the country's best for several years in his class in the K-1; he tried to teach the kids his style of paddling. Only Eric got the 'paddling bug.' The girls preferred just to feel being pushed forward by those powerful arms behind them. Klaus and I teamed up to show off our style and speed. I had also been a kayak champion in my younger years, but not quite in the same league as he was. The kids couldn't believe how fast we were. Other guests stood at the shore, shouting encouragement.

FLIGHT INTO THE UNKNOWN

There were no other boats with double paddles on the lake, only the occasional native canoe with single paddles. We explored the Flin Flon area and even the old mines open to visitors. The kids loved the one where Josiah Flintabbatey Flonatin had spent part of his life. In one area were building lots for sale, and Klaus started dreaming of owning a piece of heaven in the far north. But only Canadian citizens could buy building lots. To me, it seemed ridiculous to drive 800 kilometres to spend time in your summer cottage. Folks in Winnipeg bought one at Lake Winnipeg, Lake Manitoba, or even a bit farther away in the Whiteshell area. Many of our friends were fortunate enough to have cottages away from the city. I learned to water ski at one such weekend place and loved it.

The loons at Lake Athapapuskow got to us. Their calls touch something in your soul. It is such a shy bird, it looks more like a long duck, and it is so typically Canadian. You'll find loons on our coins, minted in Winnipeg. We were so intrigued that we took Klaus on a guided tour through the Royal Canadian Mint. A few years later, they created a one-dollar coin to replace the paper dollar. Because of the loon on one side, someone called it a Loonie and the name stuck.

Back home, one evening, I heard a scared, frightened sounding Eric calling:

"Mommy, mommy – come fast. Mommyyy, hurry up…"

He was sitting on the toilet, afraid to wipe his bum. Something was hanging out of it, a thin white string about five or six inches long. I had no idea what it was, took toilet paper, grabbed onto it and pulled. It ripped off close to his anus. I looked at it; I had never seen anything like it. I showed it to Louis.

"Heaven help, that is a tapeworm! It is still in Eric's colon. Even if you ripped off its head, it would grow a new one. You have to take Eric to the doctor! Take this thing with you."

The doctor was shocked. His explanations regarding the worm frightened me, as it could grow to five meters long, get into the boy's heart and brain and could be deadly. Eric was checked into the hospital. They starved him, feeding him only broth, grated carrots, and crushed ice to chew, they tested his stool regularly and found the worm had survived Eric's ordeal. Finally, they ordered and received medicine from Germany. Eric, my skinny boy, lost a lot of weight and was sent home seven days after he finished the pills. The doctor hoped the German medicine had done the trick. He explained how I had to check Eric's every stool, caught in a sieve in the toilet bowl, and look for pieces of this white worm. As soon as I could not detect any more of it, I was to bring that stool to the hospital lab. To Eric, he said,

"Your first fish gave you that worm. It could have killed you. The fish was probably still a bit raw when you ate it. I hope you won't give up fishing. Make sure next time the fish is very thoroughly cooked."

My fault!? I felt guilty as charged. Or not charged. My respect for worms and bugs grew. Especially for raw fish in any form. I have never eaten sushi, but oddly, sushi became one of Eric's favourite foods, and, to this day, he still loves chewing crushed ice.

FLIGHT INTO THE UNKNOWN

19: VISITING ALL GRADPARENTS IN GERMANY

My parents were able to get a visa for me to return home again, this time with my three children. We all had Canadian passports, but I was nervous. I did not forget the experience when they wanted to keep my baby boy in 1967 because he had no passport. Six years later, what would they come up with this time? It was 1973, and twenty-eight years had passed since I committed the 'criminal offence of escaping the East German Democratic Republic.'

We spent the first few days recovering from jetlag with the Bader family. Quite anxious, we boarded a train to the east, but the trip was uneventful. My parents loved having all of us there. They had changed their garden shed into a cottage with a little kitchen-living area and a bedroom. I slept soundly in my old straw bed, just like I had when I was growing up. Dad had installed a small sink; there was only cold water, but that was okay since we went swimming at the beach every day.

We helped to harvest my father's garden. He grew strawberries, raspberries, red, black, and white currants, lettuce, radishes, and peas, and he sold his produce at the campground nearby. Eric hardly ever left his Opa's side. I loved currants and had planted most of the now large bushes more than thirty years ago. I ate so many that I had to use the outhouse more than once a day. The kids fell in love with my parents and vice versa. They were old-fashioned grandparents, loving, funny, playful, cuddling.

Mom was always wearing a dress-apron and dad his old serge pants and checkered shirt. They didn't dress up like the west German grandparents, and it didn't matter when something spilled on them. Bella, my quiet girl, took longer to warm up to people. Doris was the fun-loving, outgoing, incredibly happy one. I had never seen her so happy and carefree. Everybody fell in love with her, my Aunt Irene, Uncle Heinz, and the neighbours. Eric cuddled his Omi and teased her about the loose skin on her upper arms; he called it 'blubber.' She liked the English word, not knowing what it meant. All kids loved my mom's cat, Mollie, and it was fun for them to help feed the ducks, chickens, and many rabbits. One of the bunnies became our Sunday meal.

We did not talk about it. If the kids knew, they might not have eaten it. Buying meat is fine; killing an animal known to you and eating it is a different matter. I remember! When I was fourteen, our goat Liese gave birth to two kids. They were lovely, like all babies, and I played with them. We sold one, and the other was Easter dinner. I could not eat any of it. My parents admonished me and reminded me of the time when we would have given our front teeth for any food. It was unfair. How could they expect me to eat my pet?

My kayak friends invited us to go camping with them. They had a private campground in Drigge, a forested area across the bay. Alfred, my K2 partner's husband, had a car, a Trabant, lovingly called Trabbi. People had to pay for a car in full when ordering; then they had to wait seven to ten years for delivery. Alfred picked up the kids while I paddled with Christa and all the others, just like old times. Their son Burkhardt was a few years older than Bella, but both my girls had a crush on him. Now they appreciated that we had insisted they go to German school every Saturday. They had always hated it, complaining that other kids had Saturdays off, and we have to go to the Scheiss Deutsche Schule. They were bilingual, and their skills improved each passing day. They took off into the bush with Burkhardt to do who knows what, looking for wild berries, climbing trees, but thank God not breaking any bones. They paddled with him; they laughed and flirted and enjoyed their life to the fullest.

I was happy to join the friendship regatta in the afternoon. I paddled in the K1 against my former partner Christa and other ladies. I fought the waves and won, even though I had not kayaked for more than twenty years while they had practiced every summer. The ceremony to honour the winners in the different categories had me hold my breath. Instead of me, Christa received first place mention. Eric piped up:

"I thought my mom won that race. I saw it! Why do they say Christa won?"

Alfred explained it was a friendship regatta for members only. "Your mom is not a member anymore; she paddled as a guest. She does not even live here. We are not allowed to give her a certificate."

"That doesn't seem like friendship to me." The voice of a seven-year-old.

There were about twenty paddlers. They were quiet, and one could almost cut the tension in the air. I wondered if one was a secret police informant. Everyone knew that one in every three people was one. But within my kayak friends? Damned politics.

Alfred quietly talked to Eric. We had received a sail for our paddleboat at home, but not even that cheered up the boy, he was subdued for the rest of the evening. There was music, Christa had brought her accordion, and Jorg a guitar. We sang all our old songs until late into the night, sitting around the fire pit. One after the other sport-friend disappeared, first into the bush and then into their tents. Alfred had erected one for us. This day was the best part of our holiday.

We did not have to travel to the police station in Bergen to receive our arrival and departure stamps; they were now available at the mayor's house in our village. My uncle Heinz once owned this house, but it now belonged to the state. I was surprised to meet the lady who was the postie when I was a kid. She was retired and lived upstairs. Some people at the mayor's office even remembered me as a schoolgirl. I also met my teacher, Mr. Scheider, when I showed the kids my grammar school. I had a crush on him when I was about twelve or thirteen. He complained about how wrong everything was, and that he couldn't even buy toilet paper for the school.

"It's still pieces of newspaper, Gisela, it's unbelievable, more than twenty years after you left."

During a conversation, I told my old best friend Christa how homesick I had been these past years and my longing for the olden days. We reminisced how my life would have turned out had I stayed and married one of the paddlers, or that handsome swimmer, Kurt. My mom had warned me: 'He will never be true to you, he is too attractive, and all the girls will be after him. He won't be able to remain faithful.' It hurt when Christa said,

"Gila, nobody here thinks about you the same way you feel about us."

For the train trip back to West Germany, my mom gave us a big jar of sugared strawberries. I ate most of them; the kids didn't want any. I broke out in hives. That had never happened to me, but I finished them anyway before leaving the empty jar behind on the train. My dad had given me an amber necklace as a farewell gift. I wore it under my sweater. A few tears found their way into my collar, and my children were quiet, looking at me.

Life was different at the Baders: formal, disciplined, no boisterous behaviour, but still a loving environment. I also took the children to see their maternal grandparents and to visit Doris' beloved Aunty Anna. All of them couldn't do enough for us, spoiled the children with whatever they wanted, gave them money, and sent us shopping with Aunt Anna to Frankfurt. The big busy city was overwhelming after the laid-back time in East Germany and the quiet elegance of the rural Bader home. When we entered the toy department of the large shopping centre, much larger than Eatons in Winnipeg, I had trouble keeping my crew together. Aunty told the kids they could pick whatever they wanted. We couldn't get Eric away from the Lego-City. After the toys, we went to the clothing area. I guided them a little. Bella chose a beautiful lime-green suit with a pleated skirt and fitted tailored jacket; Doris decided on a dark blue one, and each girl got a white blouse to go with it. Eric tried a pair of grey pants, a white shirt, a red vest, and a dark blue bow tie. He looked great. There were new shoes for both girls and a pair of sandals for Eric. I refused to choose anything for myself but enjoyed our tasty lunch. On the train trip back to Neu Isenburg, a short hour from Frankfurt, everyone carried shopping bags full of exciting things.

FLIGHT INTO THE UNKNOWN

Aunt Anna asked to have a private talk with me. She wanted to give me money to invest in the children's future. She thought it best not to tell Louis about it. I shook my head and said,

"I cannot keep that to myself. Why not tell him?"

"Whenever I gave Kirsten money, he took it away from her. She was never allowed to do with it what she wanted. If you tell him, he will just want it and spend it on something else. Do you think you could buy land or a house? I'll give you the down payment. Maybe you can find something with several suites you can rent out, and the rent will pay the mortgage. I'll give you $5,000 to take home. Check the market, take a good look, let me know what you can find, and I will send you more money if you need it. Gisela, I want you to know this is not just for the girls; it is for Eric too. He's a clever one."

I was speechless. What I heard about Kirsten didn't shock me. Louis had done the same to me. Undoubtedly, he would do it again, given a chance. After his bankruptcy, I had developed into a businesswoman, and couldn't be manipulated by him to the same extent. I promised Aunt Anna I would do as she requested, but Louis would have to know. I told her:

"You can rely on me; I would never, ever cheat the children out of anything meant for them."

The next day she had more news for me. She wanted me to be her heir, with the promise that whatever was left when she died, I would make sure to add it to the children's inheritance. She had her will drawn up already, and I was to go to her lawyer with her. I was incredulous, but she insisted.

"The children mean everything to me. They are all I have. And I have nobody I trust more than you."

I told her earnestly: "If this is what you want, alright. But, if you ever change your mind, feel free to do whatever you desire. I am now nearly financially independent, my business is growing, and I do not want you to think I might ever take anything for myself. If I do this, I'll do it for the children, no matter what happens."

She was like a happy child when everything was signed. "What a relief," she told me. She even added my name to all her accounts to save any inheritance tax. The bank had my written permission that she could use her money as she saw fit as long as she lived.

The Annaburg

Back in Winnipeg, after Louis got over the surprise of the unexpected money, we started to check the real estate market. It took us three weeks, and we found what we had been looking for: a house with three suites at 177 Monck Avenue, a quiet residential street lined with chestnut trees. The main floor had three bedrooms, and the second and third each had two bedrooms. A little octagonal tower was part of the upper suite, so we dubbed it the 'Annaburg.' (Fort Anna) All three suites had tenants. The asking price was $29,900. I offered $28,500, and the offer was accepted. The mortgage was about $750 a month after the downpayment of $5,000. The rent covered the taxes as well as the mortgage. Louis wasn't happy that only my name was on the owner's certificate. I told the lawyer to add 'In trust for the children.' He explained, it would cost a lot of money to create a trust but noted it in his papers. He said it wouldn't hold up legally if challenged. I thought it would never come to that anyway. I set up a separate account for the property. It was for the rent money and the expenses. I sent annual statements to Aunt Anna, who was pleased with her investment. I worked my butt off whenever there was a new tenant. Over the next few years, I painted walls and window frames, scrubbed the floors, the stoves and fridges, washed windows and even sewed curtains. I tidied up the garden and planted some shrubs and flowers in the front and backyard. My hard work kept the expenses low. In time, the income increased to over $1,000 a month. A tidy sum started to collect in the account. I loved the upper suite with the little tower room and told the children,

"When I am old, I'd like to live here."

Bella liked the main floor, Doris would move into the second, and Eric expressed his wish to live with his mother. Nobody ever mentioned Daddy. Funny; was that because he never helped us with our work on the Annaburg? He had never been there with us.

FLIGHT INTO THE UNKNOWN

About thirty years later, my grown-up son told me how he met a man who used to be our tenant. This man said to Eric: 'I have never met a woman who worked as hard as your mother did.'
.

FLIGHT INTO THE UNKNOWN

20: FRENCH ANYONE?

I registered myself for two-night school courses: I wanted to learn French and also needed to increase my knowledge of public speaking. I loved taking courses. It was a long drive from Southdale to attend the classes at Kelvin High School in River Heights, but my VW bug did not need much gas. Louis came home around 5:30 PM, and I would leave about 6:30 PM. I met another German lady, Christa Schnitzer, in my French class. She took a bus from an area halfway to my home. I offered her a ride. She had been a hairdresser in Germany and now worked out of her home. Naturally, I became her customer. One evening, coming home from school, she pointed to the sky over her house,
"Look, Giselle, the northern lights!"
Wow! I had never seen anything like it. Mostly green shapes, moving in patterns like large colourful clouds. We stood there in awe until I realized I had cold feet and better got home. I had to keep the driver-side window open during the winter to see where I was going. My little blue bug had no heat, and the windows would frost or cloud over. One night, after a heavy snowfall, a snowplow had come down Stafford Street. Leaving the warm school, I exclaimed,
"Christa, how do we ever get the car out of that snow?"
We had no shovel, but I had an idea. A bunch of young men stood there, chatting. I approached and challenged them in broken French. About a dozen of them came with me. They were able to lift my Beetle over the snow windrow with lots of fun and

laughter, all of us rolling in the snow a few times. The French class became quite enjoyable. We, two German ladies, had become part of a group and were therefore much more relaxed. The Redhead, our French teacher, was pleased that we were so eager now to learn and speak her language. I met her again when I least expected it: She was my children's French teacher.

21: A BAD ACCIDENT

It was January 31, 1974. I was on the way to a ladies' coffee afternoon at my friend Gerti's. I was in the left lane approaching a red light. A massive truck, signalling left, was in front of me. I rolled to a stop at least thirty feet behind the monster, my left turn signal also on. Eric was in a child seat harness in the back of my VW, but I did not have seat belts. I was talking to him with my head bent to the right, pointing out a sign on a charming old Real Estate building: 'Don't toss, ring Ross.' That very agency had been in our house filming a few days before. Louis wanted to list our home as soon as we found a suitable house closer to his workplace. Suddenly a larger vehicle bumped into me and shoved my car with great force under the truck. I flew against the windshield and then against the back of the seats, stretching my arm out to catch Eric. He was thrown forward and back, luckily still in his car seat. The truck had started moving.

Incredible, two police cruisers had been on the other side of the intersection. The officers saw it happen and immediately stopped everyone. They took names and addresses. The driver behind me drove a 1959 Chevrolet. He claimed he couldn't prevent sliding into me on the icy road. My car was a mess; the motor almost pushed onto the back seat. One officer stated matter of factly,

"Do you realize your car is a total write-off?" He promised to have it towed. Another police cruiser appeared and took Eric and me to the nearest hospital. The boy was okay, but I suffered severe whiplash.

The doctor, who took X-rays, explained the images and told me I was lucky to be alive. My neck would have broken had I not been sitting sideways. The first two vertebrae showed cracks. A pale, shocked Louis came to take us home four hours later. I had to wear a stiff whiplash collar for nine months, even at night. To this day, I have to move my whole upper body to look over my left shoulder. The policeman asked me,

"Do you want to sue the driver who hit you?"

Looking at the name and address, I was shocked to learn that he was the pastor of a church near where the accident occurred. How could I sue a pastor?

"I don't know, sir, I need to think about it and talk to my husband…"

I did not sue but hoped and expected the pastor to come and check on me, but he never did. I was disappointed, and I lost my respect for 'men of the cloth.'

The insurance company offered me $125 for my car. I was upset. I had paid $400 two months before the accident for a reconditioned motor. A friend gave me the name of his lawyer, who consented to take my case. I explained I had no money to pay him; he suggested he'd do it for 50% of the proceeds. I agreed. It took more than a year; I had already given up hope when I received a call from him.

"Hello, Giselle. Come to my office. I have a cheque for you."

I did not keep him on the phone because I knew lawyers charge for every minute. He had received $6,300. He had a cheque for $3,000 for me. $300 was for telephone, copies and other office supplies. I was speechless. I whispered,

"My car was not worth that much."

"No, it wasn't, but your pain and suffering, and not being able to work were worth even more. Are you satisfied?"

Yes, I was satisfied. The fact that I could have had much more if I had sued did not even enter my mind. My dear husband was pleased and already had ideas on how we would spend the money.

"Sorry, Louis, this is MY money. I have suffered for it, and I am going to buy myself a mink coat."

FLIGHT INTO THE UNKNOWN

He thought I was joking. I wasn't. I had interviewed Horst, a designer- furrier, on my TV show. Now, with money in my account, I visited his store. He showed me different finished coats, light coats and heavy coats. On my show, 'Giselle's Life Unlimited', he had asked me,

"Do you know what is the third-largest investment for a man, after a house and a car? It is a mink coat for his wife."

I had teased him. "Why a man, Horst? Can't a woman buy herself a mink coat?"

In the seventies, women did not earn much money. I couldn't even have looked at one without the accident money. Horst had also shown a great variety of fur samples on a large metal ring. He explained how the winter fur of the animals has short downy hair under the longer ones and how one can test it by blowing into it. The little mink furs are cut into tiny strips and sewn together again, not the whole pelts, nor should any part of the underbelly be used. Those parts were used to make cheaper and much lighter coats or jackets. Then he surprised me.

"Giselle, I want to design a coat, especially for you, for your sporty body type. Would you like a nearly black one? Not deep black? I have some high-quality winter pelts, and I was just waiting for the right person to order one. Don't worry. I won't charge you an arm and a leg, only material and work, no big mark-up. My design will look stunning on you, and everyone will ask you where you got your coat. You'll be a walking advertisement for me!"

I had several fittings, but could never guess the result. The next winter was just starting when I got my beautiful mink. I could set the collar in three different ways. The bottom part was a slightly fitted A-line, it had a wrap-around belt, the sleeves, widening at the wrists, were a fashion statement in themselves, following the skirt part of the coat. He had sewn the fur strips in a diagonal pattern, and Horst explained that only one designer in Montreal was able to do sleeves like that. The lining impressed me even more; the black, stitched patterned material was so beautiful that I often tried to leave my coat open to show it off. I had money left over, and Horst got most of that too. He talked me into an ermine evening jacket he would design, natural white in the style of a poncho with two rows of three-inch-long thin black monkey hair fringes around the shoulders. Monkeys are not hunted or killed; Horst had an order in for a two-inch-wide piece from every zoo around the world - in case one of those monkeys died. It took two years to get the piece of monkey fur, and he created a unique garment, the only one of its kind worldwide. It was his pride and joy, especially after he saw the Winnipeg Opera program. I was photographed, wearing it over a long black gown for the cover. It also made quite a splash when I, in the long black dress, walked down the steps from the balcony in the New York Metropolitan Opera on the arm of a handsome man.

By chance, I saw a CLOSED sign in Horst's shop window a few years later. When I enquired next door, I was shocked. Horst had died of cancer. His wife had died a year earlier, and his estate was in court. They tried finding relatives in Germany since he had left no will and had no kin in Canada. How sad, I had no idea how lonely a man he must have been.

FLIGHT INTO THE UNKNOWN

22: 83 KINGSWAY

A few days after Ross Realty filmed our house inside and out, the For Sale sign went up. Louis was secretive and suggested taking time on Sunday morning to look for a new home. Instead of driving around, he headed directly to our old neighbourhood. I asked him,

"Back to Crescentwood?"

"Yes. I liked living on Dorchester, first in the duplex, and then in Moffat's old house. It's only twenty minutes to drive from here to my work. Compare that to fifty-five minutes now from Southdale. Let's see if there's something here for us."

He turned onto Kingsway and stopped in front of number 83. A 'Private Sale' sign was next to the driveway. I shivered. It was the stately house with the four big pillars that had me wondering how people could live in something so pretentious. I had pushed Doris' doll pram with baby Eric along the sidewalk in the winter of 1965, had stopped and stared. Louis grinned when he asked me to get out of the car. We walked up to the beautiful old oak door with impressive carvings on either side. Louis had made an appointment without telling me, so we were expected. I was surprised when the door opened; I knew the owners! They owned an art shop where I had been buying art supplies for the girls' art classes after German school on Saturdays in the German Society's clubhouse. They had begged to join the art class taught by artist Mr. Potemka. Louis had been against it, I had insisted. It became an incentive to attend German school. Both girls were talented.

Entering the house, I didn't feel comfortable. We walked into a red-carpeted hallway with the walls paneled with dark wood. The red carpet and wall paneling continued up the stairway to the upper floor. The couple explained that the house was recently duplexed to help pay the mortgage. They lived upstairs. An elderly English lady, living on the main floor, hoped a new owner would let her stay. The house was built in the early 1900s. Around 1930 it became the residence of the then Premier of Manitoba, Mr. Charles D. Roblin. He was the son of Sir Rodmond Roblin and the father of the well-known Premier Duff Roblin, who now lived across the street. Duff Roblin is well known for building the Winnipeg floodway that now protects the city from flooding, the famous 'Duff's Ditch.'

The Historical Society of Canada had 83 Kingsway registered, and an owner could make changes inside but never on the outside.

After tea and conversation, we toured through the house. It had more than we needed: Kitchen, dining and living room, bathroom and two bedrooms on the second floor. Across the whole front of the house on this floor, there was a glassed-in but unheated sunroom. The third floor provided bedrooms for each child and a full bathroom. Once upon a time, these rooms had been the servant's quarters. A back stairway went from the second floor down to the main level, the cellar or the back garden. Part of the basement was finished, carpeted and had a fireplace. Next to the recreation room was a storage room.

In the adjacent part was an old furnace. It reminded me of my grandma's stone bake oven back in Pomerania. The last room was a workshop area, a workbench along one wall, and two deep tub sinks under a window, as well as a hot water tank and a washer and dryer.

What a house! It had nearly five thousand square feet of living space, not including the basement. The renter-occupied main floor suite also had two bedrooms, a bathroom, kitchen, den and living room. We needed time to think before making a decision. The children didn't want to move and change schools. Louis hoped to get them excited if they could see the house. We toured the neighbourhood with them. The grade school here was eight short city blocks away, and Kelvin High School across Stafford Street was only seven homes away.

FLIGHT INTO THE UNKNOWN

I was afraid of the higher mortgage, but Louis insisted that a mortgage is not a debt, and with the rental income, we could manage quite well. During our next visit, we agreed to buy the house. Our Southdale home sold before we could get possession of the Kingsway house. We rented a furnished apartment in a highrise for six weeks until we could move. In February, Louis flew to Germany to visit his parents; in May, we moved into our new home. Louis was happy and proud. He must have felt that he somehow caught up with his grandparents, who had lived in a similar villa. Louis designed an invitation with a picture of our 'White House' for a house-warmings party. I felt embarrassed that after his bankruptcy, we could afford a house like this and show it off.

1974 was quite a year. The girls graduated German school; the course credits were equivalent to Grade 12. Bella achieved 94%, and Doris, 97%. Each girl won a fifty-dollar prize. Eric had a few more years to attend. With more room for storage, I imported more products from Germany and started a mail-order business. My days began at 7:00 AM, and they hardly ever ended before 11:00 PM. I had developed heart problems around Christmas 1973 and was always tired since, but I kept pushing myself. Everything was too much. The children needed me, the house required my attention, and the backyard was just a large grassy area.

I befriended the English lady downstairs and, at least once a week, spent tea-time with her. She was a lonely soul. She had a niece in Kentucky, but nobody ever visited her. Dark, ugly warts covered her face and, out of embarrassment, she avoided going out. The cozy den was her favourite room. Mostly smaller paintings covered one whole wall. She kept pointing out a pretty green one with a little flower here or there. Her husband had bought it for her during a visit to London. She told me, 'It's my best. I love it so much...' I couldn't appreciate it; I liked the old Dutch Masters. She passed away a few years later, and her niece arrived from Kentucky to deal with the estate. She told me to take whatever I liked. I picked an indoor copper watering can and was too shy to ask for anything else. She hired an auctioneer to sell everything. The many pictures sold for fifty cents each. A neighbour bought the little green painting. It turned out to be an original of one of the famous GROUP OF SEVEN and was worth

$125,000, appraised by Sotheby's, the respected London auctioneers. Had she pointed out that painting to me so often, hoping I would take it? Oh, my dear God, sold for 50 cents!

The next spring's snowmelt brought more water than the Assiniboine River, a few blocks from us could handle. I came down the stairs with an armful of laundry one morning and couldn't believe my eyes. Our basement was a lake with more than knee-deep water. Louis had put extra insulation and one-meter high wood panelling around the room, it was removed when the cleanup started. I followed my nose and found a dead duck and a nest in the fireplace. We had to install wire mesh over the chimney. Several mice had also not been able to save themselves. What a mess! First, we had pumps, then huge dryers going day and night for weeks. The opening of 'Duff's Ditch' came too late for us.

I complained and told Louis, "This house is like a boat with a hole in it. We'll have to keep pouring money into it…"

There was more positive excitement for us. Germany had a military tank training base at CFB Shilo, in the vicinity of Brandon, about 200 kilometres west of Winnipeg. The German Society had invited German families and the young soldiers to an afternoon party and dance in the clubhouse. We attended with our children. I enjoyed dancing, and the young soldiers kept asking me. One wanted me to become his girlfriend. He was very interested in immigrating to Canada after his tour of duty. I laughed, and I told him I was the mother of the teenagers sitting at my table, and he should dance with one of them. He asked me,

"…and where is your husband?" When I pointed him out, the young man stopped dancing, stared at me and said,

"What? That old man is your husband? He could be your grandfather!"

A charming young devil from Berlin was also seated at our table. He danced with the girls. He had come to Canada as an exchange student. He studied dentistry in Berlin. Here, he had only found work in the construction industry. We invited him to our home. I was able to get a professor at the University of Winnipeg to write a letter stating he was working within his field to get the credits for it in Berlin. The kids, especially Eric, liked him. Wolf stayed with us often during the following years. He emptied Louis's precious liquor cabinet and even found his special hidden bottle of Scotch. He ate all the ice cream we had in our freezer. Every year, Wolf brought a different girlfriend to visit until I told him,

"You are setting a bad example for my girls. It's the last time you stay here. You need to find other lodgings."

The kids had told him a lot about Flin Flon. He went north to check it out and loved it. He was keen to buy a lot on newly developed crown land, but a foreigner could not do so. He convinced us by telephone to reserve lot # 7 in our name, and, as soon as possible, he would send us the money from Berlin to buy it. We helped him. He built a log house, and after some years, he was able to transfer it into his name. Wolf had become a successful dentist.

Klaus, my old kayak friend, came to visit with his two children. We went up to Flin Flon again. We could see but were not allowed to stay in Wolf's cabin. Wolf had bought himself some rich man's toys: A boat, a surfboard and other things, things to enjoy his holidays.

Time flew by. The house, the family, my business, my television and radio programs filled up my life. Returning from one of my B.C. promotion trips, I stopped at Lake Louise Chateau and attended a meeting of the Canadian Health Food Association. It had been founded in 1964 but was inactive. We were just a handful of people who revived it, and from then on, I was part of every meeting or convention, and always on the speaker's list. It would be too much to go into detail about it. Dr. Paavo Airola happened to be present, and a statement he made deeply hurt my feelings. We knew each other, had met at the 'alive' health retreats. He said I was not ethical because I sold skincare products for a living. Asking him where 'ethical' comes in since he made his money selling books. 'Books are intellectual, that's different.' Oh, the cheat; when we were all on a vegetarian diet at the retreat at the Emerald Lake Chateau, he got his food delivered to his cabin. A girl, working in the kitchen, had told me, 'he often orders steaks…' Well, in the long run, Karma caught up with him. That is another story.

Before I knew it, it was fall, 1976. That year put the green light on all my endeavours. The best thing that happened was the visit of both my parents. It was a wonderful time for me, as well as for the children. My father was proud to show my mother a lot of things he remembered from his first visit. He behaved like a proud Canadian. I drove to Vancouver with them and the two younger children. After several hours of driving, we weren't even in Regina, my dad asked me,

"Are we there soon, Gila?"

"No, Dad, not even a third of the way."

"Gilala, it seems like a very long trip. Think about it. We will have to go back all those many miles! Why don't you turn around now? Go back home?"

I didn't. In Germany, there was a village every few kilometres. The long highway stretching out ahead, the sheer emptiness of the Prairies, only a lonely farmhouse here or there, overwhelmed my parents. The green Province of Alberta with views of the far Rocky Mountains got them excited. They could have immigrated to Alberta in 1948, but my mother had shaken her head and refused to go. My parents were quiet when looking at the grandeur as we were driving through the Rockies. Visiting Banff and Lake Louise was almost too much for them. They had never seen any mountains in their whole life. We went up Sulphur Mountain. An indigenous older man with two long feather chief headdresses allowed people for $5 to wear one and be photographed with him. I convinced my father to do it, and he looked very much like the chief. He treasured that picture. When we finally came to Vancouver, their jaws dropped, they lost their voice. My heart overflowed with love, and I wanted to show them everything. I drove to a viewpoint on the Upper Levels Highway. We sat down on a low rock wall, overlooking the ocean to the city across the water. Both had tears running down their cheeks, so I let them be. I was shivering in dealing with my emotions.

Back at home, we told them they could stay and live in the two empty main floor suite bedrooms, with a kitchen and a bathroom. My business rented the large living room and the small den. Father was worried that he wouldn't have money for his cigars, but I convinced him otherwise. It wouldn't take long, and he would have more handyman jobs than he could handle. He was the type of man who could do just about anything. And as for mother, I wouldn't have to worry about the children. Dad wanted to stay, but mother shook her head, she was sad when she said,

FLIGHT INTO THE UNKNOWN

"If we did that, I'd never see my grandchildren at home again."

Another emotional goodbye.

FLIGHT INTO THE UNKNOWN

23: GISELLE'S PROFESSIONAL SKIN CARE

Margo, a business counsellor I had met at CBC TV, called me in spring 1976. She asked for a private meeting. Margo worked with a woman who was having difficulties with her business Just Nails Ltd. located in the upscale Tuxedo Park Shopping Centre. She wanted to rent a room for somebody like me to offer facials. I thought Just Nails was a hardware store, but no, it was the first business in Winnipeg doing false nails and fancy manicures. Their business was slow, and without my possible rental income, they would most likely have to close up. I had regular customers who came to my home studio, and as we chatted, I told Margo about some of them. I had been especially intrigued by two elderly ladies, a ninety-four-year-old and her eighty-five year-old driver friend. The ninety-four-year-old lady had come for a facial. I asked her why she seemed so excited. She told me:

"Oh, I have a date tonight, and I want to look my best. You have a way of taking ten years off with your magic hands."

"Wow, that is fantastic! So it doesn't matter how old you are, there are chances to meet guys and have fun? That gives me hope. What about sex?" I needed information regarding intimacy at an advanced age for an article I was asked to write. I was a bit embarrassed, but my lady lifted her head, looked at me and, with a cheeky expression, said,

"Giselle, it changes alright, but it never stops!"

Margo and I had a good laugh. She thought it was time for me to go commercial. She made an appointment with the owner of the nail shop. We walked into a large bright room with several manicure tables, but it still felt bare. Two small windowless rooms with doors were available for sublet. I saw a chance to start something new, made up my mind and promised:

"I am booked for several lectures and radio interviews in Vancouver in a couple of weeks. If I find a well-trained aesthetician, I will take the offer."

Vancouver had a 'European Aesthetic School.' Finding a good aesthetician in Winnipeg was impossible; the training took only three weeks during a hairdressing course. It was not enough for what I needed. European facials were not known. A Canadian facial consisted of cleansing, a mask, and make-up. European facials included a relaxing massage, removal of blackheads, special treatment for acne or rosacea and no make-up.

As had happened so often during my life when I was in dire need of something, it came to me. A young lady, working in a cosmetic studio, approached me after my sold-out lecture at the Vancouver YWCA. She was wondering if I knew of a job for her in Winnipeg. Her boyfriend had moved there, and she wanted to join him. Rose had had six months of training at the European Aesthetic School in Vancouver, plus one-year work experience. I knew her employer, and I felt guilty taking her only employee away. The young lady told me,

"I'd go anyway, even if I don't have a job. I gave my notice before you even came to Vancouver."

She could also do other services like eyebrow and lash tinting, hair removal, and manicures. The one thing she had not learned to do was pedicures. I could easily teach her that. I had taken a podiatry course in Germany. Rose became my first employee in my first commercial studio in a sublet room from Just Nails Ltd. at the exclusive Tuxedo Park Shopping Centre. I registered the new business provincially and had a sign made with the name:

'Giselle's Professional Skin Care'

Not much later, Gerda, a massage therapist at the Manitoba Winter Club, applied for a job. She had broken her shoulder nine months earlier and couldn't do full-body massages anymore. She inquired if I would be able to train her at doing facials so she could get her license.

FLIGHT INTO THE UNKNOWN

I agreed, thinking a Danish-trained massage therapist might have a trustworthy medical background. I let her watch and then spent hours evenings, Saturdays and Sundays to teach her the subtler points of doing European facials. I rented the second room from Just Nails Ltd., and they allowed me to place a sales counter and cabinet in their large front room where they did the nails. I also hired Inga, a receptionist who would answer both businesses' telephones. Inga was a former Winnipeg Carnival Princess; she loved her new job.

It was my second business. I had federally registered 'Giselle's Skindiet Cosmetic Canada Ltd.' for my wholesale/mail-order company. I had a contract with Dr. Grandel in Germany as the sole Canadian importer of their products. The packaging of all products was only in German, so I had to type - yes, on my Olympia travel typewriter - stickers with English and French translations for the dozens of imported products. It took a long time to grow my sales to the point that the company printed multi-lingual boxes for my Canadian orders. I was interviewed in Ottawa by the Ministry of Health, ask to bring relevant papers and formula proofs with me, as required. Ottawa had to approve the products. The Dr. Grandel company suggested we establish a small company. They would ship the products in larger containers; we would have to fill provided tubes and jars on location and have the boxes printed in Canada. It did not come to pass since Louis would not cooperate. They opened their first North American lab and manufacturing plant in Texas at a later date. I was a consultant and asked to offer advice. I even visited them once.

I was not allowed to advertise my business during my television program, but it did not matter. People knew me. My two staff at Tuxedo Park were busy in no time. I did not book clients for myself but visited the shop every day to make sure everything was the way I expected. My slogan was,

"If you are happy, tell others; if you are not - tell me."

Exactly one year later, the owner of Just Nails came with a friend to see me at home. They were seated, declined coffee or tea, and the owner declared,

"We came to serve you notice."

I didn't know what she meant. "Notice? Notice of what?"

"You have to vacate your business from my premises. You have four weeks to move out. We are going to start our own facial business."

I was dumbstruck. Steal my customers who were coming to this place? Isn't that underhanded? I was too polite and maybe too proud to point this out. I told them,

"I counted on a long relationship. Your business prospered with us being there, and many of my customers have also become nail customers. We complement each other."

"That's precisely it. We are ready to use all the rooms ourselves now. We have hired an aesthetician and have ordered the necessary equipment."

I had to accept the facts. I talked to Rose and Gerda and was relieved that they did not ask them to stay with Just Nails. I frantically searched for other premises nearby. Up and down every street in River Heights, nothing was suitable. I complained to my bank manager about it.

"Check across the street. There is a commercial space available above the 7-Eleven."

I signed a lease for five years – even if we didn't need so much room right now. I ordered a large sign for 'Giselle's Professional Skin Care.' Installed next to the 7-Eleven sign across the building, it made us quite visible as Academy Road was a thoroughfare. Most of the small family homes became alternative health clinics or boutique shops with handcrafted items over the next few years. I was always sorry that I didn't dare to buy one of those homes for my business.

The shocking notice I had initially thought was someone pulling the rug out from under me, now seemed like a good thing. My new salon was ready in less than four weeks. One small room became my office. We had a large reception area with three manicure stations, a sales counter, a shelving display for our products and a comfortable waiting/reading area. The larger room was divided by padded walls for body and facial treatments. I did a lot of advertising; I wrote to all my customers with the great news before we even moved. In the interim, my customers, when booking appointments at the Tuxedo location, were being told that 'Giselle's' closed forever, but they could come for service anyway. When they heard of my new site, they came back to us. It was karma when Just Nails went out of business, not even a few years later.

I hired a manager. Jerri was quick and able to take care of the bookings, organize the times, the different cabins for the various treatments, the laundry, and the daily banking at the bank across the road. In time, she could even do manicures during busy times like holiday weekends or weddings. Other than hairdressing, we were now a full-service salon, from head to toe, even make-up. Soon I had five employees. I paid everyone above minimum wage. Gerda was the only one who asked to earn commission and be allowed to book herself for after-hours or Sundays. She was middle-aged, with no family or boyfriend, only a Great Dane. Myself, Jerri and Gerda were the only keyholders.

As was the law, I paid Unemployment Insurance and the company portion of the Canadian Pension Plan for all. I was not required to pay it for commission earners, but out of consideration, I did for Gerda. If her shoulder problem gave her trouble, she could at least apply for Unemployment Insurance. She never needed it. A year later, she left and started her own business a few blocks from us. I did not have to pay holiday pay for commission earners, but she went to the labour board, complained and won - because I had paid Unemployment and into the Pension Plan for her. Being too considerate backfired on me.

One Sunday afternoon, I was shocked to find the shop door open. There had been a break-in. Since the bank closed on Saturdays, the day's take had been inside. It was gone. Otherwise, everything looked all right. I called the police and arranged an emergency locksmith to install a new lock. Arriving Monday morning before everyone else, I had another shock. Blood all over the public stairs and on the walls. Had someone been murdered? I felt shaky. Four teenage boys sat on the steps further up, sipping Slurpees, looking a bloody mess as well. Teenagers were a problem we couldn't fix - it was a public stairway, with 7-Eleven downstairs. When I approached the teens, asking about the blood, they had a laughing fit. I was annoyed and warned them I would call the police. They couldn't stop laughing, explaining it was all due to a ketchup fight.

"Don't get your knickers in a knot, lady, we are okay. We just had a bit of fun."

I didn't want them to hold a grudge against me, so I laughed with them. Had these youngsters broken into my shop? I tried a few round-about questions, but they didn't seem to know anything about it.

Getting a pail with water and a rag, I asked them to clean up the mess, and they did. As each employee arrived, I told them about the break-in. I asked Jerri,

"Please, come with me. I want to climb inside the big garbage bin behind the building."

" You? Why would you want to do that?"

"I am thinking like a thief. I have a feeling the cheques for the deposit might be in there. The thieves couldn't use them."

I found all the cheques that had been in Saturday's deposit bag. Only the cash was missing. Since I had reported it to the police on Sunday, it was fully insured.

FLIGHT INTO THE UNKNOWN

24: NEW YORK - NEW YORK

I was over the moon when I received an invitation to be the luncheon speaker at a conference of the editors of women's and related magazines in New York for November 1976. New York! Me - in New York?! After the initial excitement, I questioned myself: Was I good enough? Editors of Vogue and many other famous magazines would be present. What could I tell them? Would I stutter? Would I forget everything I was going to say? Would I faint? Would they laugh at me? Or walk out? Had they made a mistake by inviting me?

There was a telephone number for Caroline, the lady who organized it. I called her. She told me,

"No, there is no mistake. You have exciting new ideas; just be yourself. You have a name on radio and TV in Canada, and conference organizers like us picked up on you. Prepare yourself for twenty to thirty minutes. There will be about a hundred people attending, give or take. Will you accept it? Great, I'll make the arrangements. You'll be staying at the Waldorf Astoria Hotel. The conference will be at the Sheraton Hotel; a limousine will be available for you. Come to New York a few days before the meeting. Make time for a tour of New York and maybe some shopping. Inform me of your arrival and departure times."

It was easy to talk to Caroline. I felt as if we knew each other, and my excitement tripled. Louis was proud of me and even a little jealous. Within days, I received a letter from Dr. Grandel's company. They were going to send two representatives and become a sponsor of the conference. The reps were their chemist, Mr. Niemann, and the new man for international relations, Mr. Gronsten. They would also stay at the Waldorf.

The flight from Winnipeg stopped in Montreal before continuing to New York. I was pretty nervous and wondered if the limousine would be waiting for me. I talked to the stewardess, and she shared my excitement. A liveried chauffeur, holding a sign with my name, was at the gate. On the way downtown, he tried to make conversation, but I was in no mood for it. I sat in the back of the car and often met his eyes in the rearview mirror. With several hours of the time difference in addition to the flying time, I was tired, and it was starting to get dark. After check-in at the hotel, I contemplated staying in my room, but curiosity got the better of me. The Waldorf Astoria often appeared in romance novels, and I wanted to see as much of it as I could.

I saw the two gentlemen from Germany. They sat at the bar and invited me to join them for dinner. I looked around at the other guests and asked myself: How many of them would be at my presentation? We contemplated what to do the next day. Mr. Gronsten had plans, Mr. Niemann, the chemist I had worked with years ago to develop new skin care products, asked me if I would be up for a visit to the Metropolitan Opera. Enthusiastically, I said yes. I had planned to go and had even brought the required outfit. I felt much more comfortable having a companion. The three of us decided to visit the Rockefeller Centre the next evening jointly. Tony Bennett would be singing.

I met with Caroline, the friendly organizer, in the morning. She wanted me to feel more at home with the setting and gave me pointers for my presentation. There was an interview with a newspaper journalist. Radio and TV media would be present during lunch. Caroline's advice:

"Once you are introduced and start speaking, don't worry if the attendees continue chattering and making noise with their cutlery, just keep talking. They listen with one ear, and when they catch something of interest to them, they stop. I'm sure you'll get their attention."

She surprised me with a complimentary city tour. Another limousine picked me up, a much larger one with four seats facing each other and a well-stocked bar in the middle. The driver closed the glass partition to the front part of the car, but he could talk to me anyway. He encouraged me to have a glass of champagne, wine, or whatever I liked. He told me about the areas we passed, from the Bronx to 42nd Avenue; the highlight was a visit to the Twin Towers. He made a phone call when we arrived. He delivered me to a uniformed guide in one of the towers. This man took me into an elevator up to the top. What a view! I could tell he enjoyed being my guide since I was an attentive guest.

He answered all my questions; he knew a lot of details about New York and the buildings I could see. He also took me past several offices to witness financial transactions and other exciting goings-on. I had a glimpse into a life I couldn't even imagine. We finished this tour in an exquisite café with a coffee and an éclair. My chauffeur waited to continue the journey and insisted I go into Bloomingdales, Tiffanys and another famous shop on 5th Avenue. I went to look, but I didn't buy anything, I was way too nervous. I was treated like somebody, but I also thought I was a nobody in the overwhelming city of New York.

We enjoyed Tony Bennett in the evening. He sang Christmas songs and finished with my favourite: 'I left my heart in San Francisco…' The Rockefeller Centre was packed with people. Later, back in bed at the Waldorf, I felt like a fairy princess in a dream. Will I wake up in the morning and be back in Winnipeg? But it got even more exciting.

We arrived early at the Sheraton. Outside the conference room was a row of coat stands; they were already tight with coats and jackets. I did not feel comfortable leaving my fur here, but the attendee convinced me that it was safe. The lunchroom had linen-clad tables beautifully set with china, silver and crystal glasses. The final number of attendees: One hundred and ten, men and women, but naturally more women editors. It was just as Caroline had predicted. It was not quiet after my brief introduction. I followed Caroline's advice and just kept on speaking, acting with my voice, getting softer and louder, and as I was getting annoyed with their indifference after a few minutes, I expressed my mind. I was getting passionate about my topic,

"Look Younger as the Years Go By!"

Within seconds, the room was quiet. I could hear the scratching of pens on paper. I told them that makeup is only a mask, but could be used to underline attractive features and went on to explain that true beauty comes from within. Food choices are essential. Being embarrassed to ride a bike, once you are a grown-up in North America, is ridiculous. Exercise in all its forms, from walking to dancing, swimming to jogging, or riding a bike instead of using a car, will help you look younger and healthier. A healthy body will have a significant effect on the state of your skin, as it is the largest and also the only organ you can see. I talked about water, how it can be used either cold, warm or even as steam or ice. I mentioned the different types of sauna and how regular use affects the skin. I finished with

"To be truly beautiful, you have to change your lazy, comfortable lifestyle to an active one. Don't take the car to the letterbox; walk every chance you have!"

There were lots of questions at the end. The chairperson finally cut it off. I had spoken longer than anticipated. I didn't get a standing ovation, but plenty of applause. People came rushing to me, wanting more - but Caroline took me to the media room. Several radio stations did ten-minute interviews with me, and before I knew it, a TV reporter took me by the arm. Off we went into an elevator to another floor, occupied by several TV stations to be interviewed on several programs. I was in my element. I was not afraid or nervous anymore. I was telling them the way I saw it. They loved it. It had been several hours since I had left my fur coat by the conference room. I finally remembered and wondered what might have happened to it. When I returned to that floor, it was gone. Everyone else was gone as well. I sat down on a lonely chair, deflated and was about to cry when Mr. Niemann came around the corner with my coat over his arm.

"When we couldn't find you anywhere, I thought I better save it for you," he said. "I knew you would turn up here to pick it up."

We took a taxi back to the Waldorf. I needed a rest to de-stress before an early dinner and before dressing up for the Metropolitan Opera in a long black gown with my white ermine jacket with the black monkey hair over my shoulder. I never wore makeup, just a touch of lipstick; I was glowing from within. Mr. Niemann wore black tie and looked very handsome. We had seats in the first row of the first balcony. If my memory serves me right, the performance was 'Aida.' Coming down the stairs during intermission, people were staring at us. We were a striking looking pair. I could almost see the gears turning in their heads: Who are these two?

What a finish to this day! The next morning, packing my suitcase, I heard a knock on my door. It was Mr. Niemann. He told me they had booked the airport shuttle, the three of us would go together. We still had time for a quick lunch as the shuttle would leave in about two hours. We started chatting about old times in Augsburg. I told him that I had quite a crush on him at the time and that our boss, Dr. Grandel, had picked up on it. He had teased me that I shouldn't get any ideas because Mr. Nieman is very much married.

Mr. Nieman started laughing. It startled me, and I stopped packing, looking at him.

"What's so funny?"

He got up, took my head between his hands, looked into my eyes and said,

"What's so funny? You and I are funny. I was totally in love with you back then, but you were always aloof and professional. I never realized that you even liked me. I had told my wife about you, and it was she who helped me get over it."

He kissed me. It was the first and only time a kiss made me feel soft in the knees like heroines experienced in novels. It had never happened to me, and I knew, if I would not untangle myself right now, it might lead to more. I softly pushed him away, took a deep breath and bent low over my packing. I did not want him to see my face; I felt so weak. He understood. After all, we were both married. If I hadn't been, I would never have told him about those feelings of the past. He stayed for a few more minutes, helped me close the suitcase, picked it up and then said as if nothing had happened,

"Are you going to have a bite with us? Come down when you are ready. You know where we will be. "

I was amazed when he, sitting next to me in the shuttle, took my hand and held it for the whole trip to the airport. He didn't seem to care that Mr. Gronsten saw it. I was embarrassed, but I didn't pull my hand away. I boarded my plane to Winnipeg, and they went to a different gate for their departure to Germany. I met his wife a year later when I was in Augsburg for an international conference. I wondered if he had told her about the kiss in New York, but I never asked. The three of us became good friends for many years. They had a dachshund but no children. Every time I was in Germany, I visited with them. He died a few weeks before his retirement, bent over his desk. He had concealed that he was suffering from cancer and worked to his last breath.

New York was one of the highlights of my life. It was the beginning of exciting years to follow. Articles started to appear in magazines approximately three months after my talk. Many writers used my words but never mentioned my name. It seemed I had unwittingly started a fitness craze, with many new gyms and spas opening. Eventually, it developed into what became known in Canada as 'Participaction.'

25: BACK DOWN TO EARTH

It wasn't easy to get back into my ordinary life after flying so high in New York. C'est la vie! My salon was always fully booked. I invited my employees for a Christmas party at my home. I had thoughtful gifts for each one, and they told stories about experiences with customers. Everyone was looking forward to another good year.

This Christmas, my gifts for my family were grand: Five sets of cross-country skis, poles, mitts, and toques and a holiday week in Banff, Alberta. I had also bought our first colour television. Their reaction? The kids would rather stay at home to watch TV, instead of travelling and doing things they had never done before. Sadly, that's what the girls did in Banff. They watched TV in their room while Louis, Eric, and I went out with our skis. It was upsetting trying to get them to ski. We gave up. After all, it was Christmas. Two sets of skis had been a total waste of money.

New Year's Eve was something else. We had a reservation for the Medieval Dinner in the beautiful old castle-like Banff Springs Hotel. Straw-covered floors, waiters and waitresses dressed in medieval clothing, medieval music, no tablecloth, and only a knife for cutlery. On long tables were platters with steaks and chicken pieces; you took what you wanted, ate with your fingers. Weird, but we just threw the bones onto the floor. No social graces were required. It was a new experience. Eric was really into it and clowned around with the servers.

Bella graduated from high school in 1977. We talked about university and asked her what she wanted to study. Bella did not want to go to university but wanted to attend the European Aesthetic School in Vancouver. I argued that she was too smart not to do more with her life, but Louis gave in.

"If that's what you want… maybe you are too stupid for university anyway."

I had a big fight with him later that evening. We frequently had arguments during the last year, and it was always about the girls. He put them down while I tried to build their self-esteem, remembering how I had to struggle to get an education. Why shouldn't they have a better life? It was so easy - why not take advantage of it? Louis usually shut me down with,

"I grew up during the war. I was only fifteen when conscripted to fight the enemy, and I made my life without a university education. If Bella wants to be an aesthetician, she can work in your salon. She sees easy money after only one year."

Bella left us for a year in Vancouver, the city where she was born. She loved it. By now, I was a member of the International Cosmetology Association. I attended a meeting in London. I spoke at an international convention where I made contact with the British Dr. Grandel importers, a couple who lived some hundred kilometres away. They had invited me to their home for a few days, and I accepted. It was my first ride in a chauffeur-driven Rolls-Royce. The men sat in front, the lady and I in the back. It was a comfortable car, but I could not enjoy the ride because both men smoked. The air in the car was blue with smoke.

They lived in the 'Sheriff's House' a sizeable Tudor-style building, somewhere in Norwich. They had been able to buy it because nobody else had wanted it. It was a haunted house; the Sheriff, long dead, made regular, troubling appearances. A small guesthouse was next to it. Several of their guests had left after seeing a ghost, a lady in white. Had I seen her too? I wasn't sure. Did I dream that I saw her standing at the door to my room? The couple owned a beautiful Dalmation dog; it joined me on my daily walks in their park with a river the natural border. People in small boats coming by would wave to us, and I felt like a heroine in a novel, standing there with long (borrowed) boots in my camel-coloured pantsuit, the dog at my side. I took the train back to

FLIGHT INTO THE UNKNOWN

London and spent another couple of nights there before I flew home.

In London, I visited a small lane of antique shops. I was able to buy a Victorian watch like English nurses used to wear pinned on their aprons. The lady in Norwich had been a nurse; she wore one on the lapel of her blazer. I had admired it. Mine is even prettier, it is 14-carat gold with blue Roman numerals on a white face, surrounded with diamonds.

The famous Harrod's department store was not far. I walked over, browsing until I found what I was looking for: Ladies' clothing. A woollen coat was displayed high up on a wall, patterned with small black and beige squares, a hood, a generous cut. It was my size. I bought it and wore it on my flight home. It was fun to stand next to my waiting family, and they hadn't recognized me.

In 1978, Louis and I went on a holiday to Martinique, the birthplace of Napoleon's first wife, Empress Josephine. We visited the Josephine museum; there were lots of letters from Napoleon. One tickled my funny-bone. He wrote beautiful love letters. Unfortunately, his later marriage to the Habsburg princess was not a happy one. It was a political marriage; he had divorced Josephine and married her to father an heir with royal blood - which he didn't have. The letter I'm referring to read like this:

"Don't wash – I'm on my way." (English translation)

Touring the island, we came across a statue of Josephine. Somebody had cut off her head. It was never recovered or replaced. Martinique is not an island I'd go back to, but our visit was enjoyable. One excursion to a village covered in up to thirty meters of volcanic ash from an eruption in 1902 was quite frightening. The guide explained that most villagers were buried alive underneath it since it happened fast and without warning.

Bella finished her aesthetic training in Vancouver, and Doris graduated from high school. Her grades were superb. Surely she would go to university. To my disappointment, she insisted on also becoming an aesthetician, enrolling at a new cosmetic school in Edmonton since the one in Vancouver was full. No argument from us could persuade her to change her mind. She even accused me of favouring Bella, and shouted,

"It's always Bella, Bella, Bella! Why not me? She always gets what she wants, why not me?"

Again, her dad made a sarcastic remark, and she got what she wanted.

For the summer of 1978, I planned to take Eric and Doris with me to East Germany. My parents had sent me a visa to visit in July. Doris did not want to go, so I went with Eric. He always had a great time with his cousin Arne, who was a year younger. Eric wanted to stay in East Germany because the girls are much prettier and more agreeable than in Canada. He sure had a way with the ladies!

I wanted Eric to have the best education possible. I made an appointment with a professor at the University of Winnipeg; they had a collegiate that offered high school classes. I had met this gentleman a few times at social gatherings. He hugged me and proceeded to make sexual advances. I backed off and told him this is not why I came. He took a few steps back, looked me up and down and said,

"Who do you think you are? High-nosed, eh? There are lots of women above your station, you know them, and they all do it."

"Well, I don't." I turned and left. What is it with men in positions of power? Why do they think they can have any woman? I can't trust men anymore. He was not the first one who tried.

I enrolled Eric in the prestigious St. Johns Ravenscourt school in Winnipeg for the school year 1978/79. Everybody who was somebody, lawyers, doctors or politicians, was a graduate of Ravenscourt. I was doing a lot of national and international travel for my business, and therefore, I thought it best he boarded at the school during the weekdays and came home only on weekends. I was proud to be able to afford to have my son at the best school he could ever attend. He didn't like to be away from his buddies for the whole week - but he had no choice in the matter.

In spring 1979, Louis and I went on a holiday to Barbados. We stayed in a cute hotel right on the beach with incredibly fine white sand. They also had a pool. I felt like a dwarf since the Barbadians, especially the men who served us, had fantastic figures and were very tall. Since I do not like air-conditioning, we had left our bedroom window open at night. During the third night,

FLIGHT INTO THE UNKNOWN

I woke up choking. My bed was the closest to the window, but Louis tasted dust as well, looked out the window and whispered,

"Something is going on out there. It looks like they put a black cover over the pool, there's a lot of activity with people shouting. Do you want me to phone the operator and ask to send us a doctor?" He closed the window and looked at his black hands, not comprehending.

I could only nod. It took a while for the operator to answer. "Please, keep the line free. We have an emergency. There's been a volcanic eruption on St. Vincent, a neighbouring island. It's ninety miles away, but the wind is blowing the ashes our way."

"But my wife is choking. We need a doctor."

"Do not open any windows. We'll send one. The doctor is already in the hotel."

The doctor suggested going to the hospital. He recommended an operation to open my airways. What, a slit in my neck? No way.

"I'll deal with it. I'll rinse my mouth and gargle. I'll not go outside…" and I thought, "I'd rather die."

It was a frightening night. We were in a building across from the reception and dining rooms. Holding wet washcloths over our mouth and nose, we walked over for breakfast. Except for a scratchy throat, I felt almost normal again. Not only was the pool unusable, but also the beach and the chairs, everything was black. I joked with the dark-skinned Barbadians about really blending in, and they laughed. They worked feverishly, trying to get pathways, doors and windows cleaned. We left footprints in the ashes, and ours were not the only ones.

We had to take our shoes off when entering any buildings. We stayed five more nights but this holiday was not one we enjoyed.

The alive magazine had advertised and organized a weeklong health retreat at the Emerald Lake Chateau. Naturally, I participated again. The Emerald Lake Chateau had a new owner; for the next time, we needed another venue. Sadly, we couldn't find anything suitable in the area, so this was our last retreat.

A month later, I went car shopping with Eric. Despite his young age, he knew a lot about cars. He was excited about an Italian-designed special edition Volvo Bertone Coupé. Eric knew about Volvos' reputation and quality related to the Swedish airline industry. The Coupé was elegant and smelled of new leather; it looked and felt expensive. I couldn't stand it - gold with a champagne interior. It seemed oppressive to me. Eric liked it, but he was not against checking out the Mercedes-Benz dealership. As we drove up, Eric spotted a single white car sitting on an otherwise empty lot, not far from the building.

"Hey, Mom, there is your car!" As I parked, he jumped out and ran right over to the automobile. I followed, and as we looked it over, a salesman joined us. You guessed it - I bought the car. The Mercedes was a 240 Diesel, had a dark blue interior and felt good. The price was $23,000 plus $300 tax, and they gave me a satisfactory trade-in value for my Mercury. The salesman told me:

"Always remember, a Mercedes is not an expense; it is an investment."

Who would believe that! For me, driving a Mercedes was a statement that 'I have arrived.' I couldn't wait to send a photo to my father; he would have tears in his eyes and would be so proud of me. Back in my office, I asked my secretary to phone Louis and ask him to buy a bottle of champagne. She was not allowed to tell him why, she only said, "Giselle has something to celebrate." My accountant happened to be at my office that day to do the books.

The salesman had affixed a couple of small roses to the star hood ornament. When Louis drove up the driveway and saw my new car, I knew he was unhappy. To avoid letting him drive it when his car was in service, I also bought a Volkswagen Beetle for the business. Doris soon had an accident with it, nothing too dangerous. A few years later, Bella bought it for the low book value.

Not much later, Louis and I went and bought him a Cadillac Seville. Except for the trade-in value for his dodge, I paid for it. He promised that in return, his Liechtenstein Stamp collection would be mine. I never did get it.

In retrospect, 1979 was a hectic year. Eric and I flew to Germany again in August. I had a meeting with the Grandel company and wanted to see my parents again. Towards the end of the year, my health was declining. I seriously considered selling my retail business, but it was not a seller's market.

For Christmas, we visited Barbara, Louis's youngest sister, in Chicago. She had married a wealthy man and lived in a beautiful house in Hinsdale. He mentioned to me,

FLIGHT INTO THE UNKNOWN

"I have the money, but Barbara added the class."

He belonged to the Chicago Mercedes-Benz Club, and we all attended their New Year's party. Big game trophies from Africa mounted on the walls made me think they were all hunters. In a transparent display case was a big black, hairy live tarantula, it gave me the creeps. A funny leathery thing about four or five feet long and a foot wide at one end, hanging horizontally over the bar, caught my eye.

"What is that thing?" I asked the bartender. He looked at me and laughed:

"That, my lady, is the penis of a Rhinoceros."

FLIGHT INTO THE UNKNOWN

26: PRINCE CHARMING

After coming home from the Chicago festivities, I was exhausted. I worked frantically to catch up with the inventory for the year-end. I was so tired that I almost fell over my own feet. One day, as I waited for a teller at the bank, someone behind me tapped my shoulder.

"Oh! Hi Carol! I didn't know you banked here." Carol was our travel agent.

"Probably longer than you, Giselle. How's business?"

"Ah, pretty slow... we just finished our year-end inventory. Counting those hundreds of items is not fun."

It was early January. Every day the temperature was below freezing. For several weeks now, people have shivered through thirty below zero.

Carol laughed. "You look tired, ready for a holiday. Why don't you come with me to Jamaica? I'm taking a small group to Montego Bay. One seat's still available."

"Jamaica? Boy-oh-boy, Carol, what a dream to get away from this cold! When are you going?"

"Tomorrow."

"You must be kidding! I couldn't possibly go tomorrow. What would I tell my husband? And my business..."

"Come on, Giselle, where there's a will, there's a way. Tell your husband you're going to Jamaica tomorrow, bingo. Your secretary has looked after your business before. We don't have to be at the airport until 6.00 in the evening. You have a whole day to get organized. Plus, you have the rest of today."

Thoughts of swaying palm trees and a white sandy beach went through my mind. I could almost feel the sun on my back.

"How long are you going for?"

"Two weeks. Tell you what. Go home and think about it. Call me later today. I'll keep that seat open for you, o.k.?"

While driving home, I knew already I was going to go. I couldn't pass it up. The price was right; inventory finished, bookings at my studio after Christmas and New Year were sparse. January was never busy. My secretary said, 'go.' When Louis got home from work, he found me in the bedroom, packing a suitcase.

"What are you doing? Going somewhere?"

"Yes. Carol has a small group going to Jamaica tomorrow. She offered me the last seat on the plane. Don't be mad. I really need a holiday."

"Mad? Why should I be mad? I am glad you are going! Lately, you have been hard to live with. It will do you good."

Wow. That was easy! When I phoned Carol, she only said, "I knew you'd come."

To say the next day was busy is an understatement. I was at the airport at 6 PM to meet the group, half an hour later we were airborne. I was exhausted and fell asleep in my seat in first class, next to Carol. It was a super flight, holiday-ish! By 10:30 PM, we were dancing under the stars. Who would want to go to bed? Miss the inspiring Caribbean music? See and join all the laughter?

There were games. First time I experienced turtle races. The little creatures had a red, blue, yellow, green, or white spot painted on their back. There was a wooden ring around a sandy circle, about five feet diameter. The turtles, dumped into the centre, started running in all directions. People would bid on their colour and hoped it would be the first to the edge. Everybody was shouting to encourage their turtle, but they would start, stop, turn around, go in a different direction, go back to the middle; it was quite nerve-racking. At first, I thought it was silly but then began shouting too.

In the second round, I sponsored the white one, and my turtle won. I received a tropical Jamaican drink, laced with dark rum. Yummy. I wasn't used to alcohol and could feel its effect right away. I felt daring and signed up for a different game, two long poles, each end held by a squatting person. They clapped the poles together to the rhythm of the music, and one had to hop between them, in and out, trying not to get hit. Of four participants, I was the last one still jumping when the music stopped. I had won another of those delicious drinks. I didn't decline it - I enjoyed it. Was I tipsy? Maybe, but I felt pretty happy.

Several couples were dancing. I looked around for any single men. None! The next dance didn't require a partner. A handsome Jamaican devil taught a Reggae dance. I joyfully participated, caught on quickly. I hoped they would do more dances for singles. But they didn't.

I felt sad. Suddenly, a man in front of me held out his hand, and I jumped for the chance to dance. I considered myself a good dancer, but I had no idea that I could dance like THAT! The drinks had loosened me up, and I followed the man's every move, and all of a sudden, we had the whole dance area to ourselves. Imagine, the Jamaican steel drums, the warm night, the stars, the laughter, moving like a feather in a breeze, the encouraging clapping, I wished it would never end.

The typical last piece the band played was 'Good Night, Irene.' My Prince Charming leaned over my hand and disappeared. We had never spoken a word.

The days were dreamlike. I enjoyed the beach and swimming. I made friends with a Jamaican lady who came by every so often, carrying a huge basket of tropical fruit on her head. The basket weighed eighty pounds, but she moved as if she wore a gigantic hat. I bought different types of fruit every morning. She introduced me to sweet sap and sour sap, and each looked like a flat cactus; I tried a purple apple that looked like a pear and tasted like a plum. After a few days, she told me about herself. Three kids and all had a different father.

"Are you married to one of them?"

"Married? I'm not crazy! Haven't you seen all the Jamaican men sitting around all day in black pants and white shirts? Smoking and drinking? Why would I marry one of them? They enjoy life, and we women have to work to bring home the money. Not me. I work for myself and my kids. If I want sex, I can have that without being married. I'm no cook or doing washing for anyone else."

She told me a lot about Jamaican life. It surprised me to learn that they use marijuana leaves for cooking and in salads. "No big deal," she said, "We grow it in our veggie garden. It's healthy."

One day, we had an excursion to Negril to visit a famous bar on a cliff. Jamaican guys were diving from dizzying heights down into a pool of water. As we approached, I smelled something strange. Something never encountered before. I inhaled deeply and exclaimed,

"Aaaah! What's that smell?" It was different. I looked around, but there were no flowering bushes.

"What? Have you never smoked it?" That was the voice of our driver.

Every evening the steel band would play, games were going on, and I was waiting and looking out for my Prince Charming. As a man, he was not my type, but as a dance partner, he was unbeatable. He always arrived late, danced a few times with me, smiled, but we had no conversations. On the fourth evening, I asked him,

"How come you are such an incredible dancer? I'm Giselle. Mind telling me your name?"

"I'm Gerard. My German partner Horst and I own a dance studio in Holland."

No wonder, I thought, a dance teacher!

"We leave tomorrow. Sorry to disappoint you. Horst is afraid you'd fall in love with me. I'm gay, you see."

I did not understand. "Gay? We are all happy and gay, Gerard. We are on holiday and enjoying the fun."

"Giselle, I meant gay in another way. Horst has become quite upset with me. He cut our holiday short. I think he is jealous. He doesn't dance and is always watching us from behind those bushes."

"Oh. It doesn't matter to me. Tell Horst; he doesn't have to worry about me, I am married. I just enjoy dancing with you." After the dance ended, I thanked him for teaching me so much and wished him and Horst a safe flight home. Smiling, I didn't show my disappointment.

FLIGHT INTO THE UNKNOWN

The next morning, I walked the paved trail along the ocean towards the airport. A low wall separated it about a hundred meters from the runway. People would be sitting there, watching flights take off and disappear over the ocean. I sat down and contemplated my life. Funny, it was always so hard to leave home, and now it seemed so far away, it didn't even matter if I ever went back. I'd find a job here, maybe even in our hotel. A young boy, probably about ten or eleven years old, came and sat a few feet from me. After a while, he asked,

"Are you sad, lady?"

I looked at the friendly Jamaican kid and nodded.

"Is it your husband? No Problem! My mother told me that husbands are shitholes. She taught me how to make you happy. Do you want to do it down at the beach, or do you want me to come to your hotel?"

I was speechless. Shocked. Was this one of my fruit lady's kids? Just then, three white men stood up, heading in the direction of my hotel. I jumped up and followed them. One turned around and asked me,

"Is something wrong?"

"Yes," I said, "it's the Jamaican lifestyle. The answer to everything is No Problem!" The four of us laughed and wandered on.

The two weeks with Carol's group were up. I went to the office to phone my secretary. Before I could ask, she said,

"If you have enough money on your Visa card, stay where you are, Giselle. There are no bookings. Nobody's leaving their home. We are having a Siberian cold wave and masses of snow."

I decided to let my return ticket go to waste. I stayed for another week. A German group of nine people took me under their wing. They sunbathed topless. On the second or third day, one lady commented,

"You never take your top…"

Before she finished speaking, I reached behind me, unhooked it, and it was off. I have a photograph showing nine evenly tanned people, and me with a white chest.

Prince Charming being gay, a young boy wanting to make me happy, a woman telling me a lot about her island life, experiencing topless suntanning and swimming - I came home a different woman.

'Jamaica? No Problem!.' Paying for an extra week at the hotel and a new return ticket was the best gift I ever made to myself!

FLIGHT INTO THE UNKNOWN

27: DARK CLOUDS ON THE HORIZON

Working became a real chore for me. I kept pushing myself but was always tired. I had to attend to my import wholesale business with a secretary. I was dealing with mail orders and shipping products to stores across Canada; I had my retail store and skin care salon with half a dozen employees, now also employing my daughter Bella. I did my regular live television program, which the TV station taped and showed four more times each week at different hours; I was a frequent guest on TV and radio stations across the country. I was a sought after speaker for all Canadian and US natural health conventions. My name became synonymous with alternative health, skincare and beauty. One radio announcer called me a 'walking encyclopedia when it comes to healthy living.' I wrote for several Canadian and US magazines; newspapers interviewed me, and to this day, I kept two thick folders with all the clippings from those years when I was flying so high.

I often thought about my holiday in Jamaica and how good I felt. I booked again, and this time I invited Bella to come with me, my gift for her 21st birthday. She enjoyed it a lot, met other young people, and went to parties. I told her,

"I trust you. Don't do anything I wouldn't do..."

She usually laughed, and when she came home to the hotel told me how much fun she'd had. One night, she whispered,

"Mom, I met Sylvester Stallone. He likes me. But I'm so tall, and he is so short. He says it doesn't matter."

"You are kidding! Bella, I can't believe that - I wouldn't trust an actor. A boxer!"

She giggled and told me the next night that it wasn't the real Sylvester, just a look-alike. For some reason, she didn't want to go out for a few days. Now we did a lot of things together.

Bella, my tall girl with the shoulder-length medium-blond curly hair, was noticed by men, especially the Jamaican men. I told her of my experience with the ten-year-old boy who wanted to make me happy and warned her. It was a lovely holiday for the two of us, and I still treasure my photo album. Doris would turn twenty-one the following year in May, and it would be her turn to come with me.

Later that spring, I drove from Winnipeg with stops in Regina, Saskatoon, Edmonton, Vancouver, and, on the way back, in Kelowna. In each city, I stopped for interviews on TV, radio and several newspapers. The journalist in Saskatoon did not believe in 'natural' and tried to give me a hard time. I became quite passionate und was surprised to see a full page of the interview and a large picture of myself with an intense expression in his paper the next morning. As was my custom, the day after a public appearance, I would be available for consultation at the shops that carried my products. Sometimes I had line-ups so long that my visits went late into evening hours. The shops didn't mind. My presence significantly increased their sales, and not just my skincare line. My motto was 'Skincare from the Inside Out' - and that meant that I always recommended a healthy diet or change of lifestyle, a common approach today, but avant-garde in those days.

I knew the owners of the Kelowna shop. They invited me to stay with them instead of in a hotel. They had a light-brown miniature poodle named Cindy. Cindy stayed close to me, put her paw on my knee, looking at me as if she was going to ask or tell me something. I fell in love with her and expressed my sentiments to my friend Lorie,

"If you - for any reason - ever want to give up this poodle, I'll take her any day!"

I meant it in jest. We never had a dog. I had no idea how my family would react to it. I never even mentioned it. A few weeks later, Lorie called me.

FLIGHT INTO THE UNKNOWN

"Giselle, did you mean it when you said you would take Cindy? Gord and I are splitting up. None of our grown children want or can take her. If you are not serious, we'll have her put down."

What a shock. Had Cindy already known that when she befriended me? Was that what she was trying to tell me? Had she picked me as her next owner? These thoughts went through my head. I knew I had to take her. I wanted to take her. I did not tell my family. Lorie explained she would put her in a dog kennel and ship her by air to Winnipeg. Cindy will be sedated for the flight and arrive an evening after supper. I told my family that we had a visitor, and we should go to the airport to pick her up. I didn't answer any questions about who it was. I just promised, 'someone you'll love.'

All five of us were waiting, and once every passenger had gone, we were the last ones. The kids were disappointed. Then a man came carrying the kennel, Cindy lying in it, looking out of dull eyes when I bent down.

"What? Mom, a doooog? Why didn't you tell us? Oh, the poor thing, look at her – can we keep her? Please, Mom, can we keep her?"

We took her home, made a place for her in the corner of the kitchen. When she came to, she needed to pee, but we didn't understand that she wanted to go out. She did it on the kitchen floor and seemed very embarrassed. Eric was quick to clean it up. When we went to bed, I heard her cry. Poor Cindy, I thought, you find yourself in strange surroundings. Eventually, it was quiet. I had no idea that Eric had taken his pillow and blanket and slept with her on the floor. I found them the next morning cuddled up together. We all loved Cindy. She was a ray of sunshine. She quickly learned what we expected of her. I started running with her every morning. I would wash her paws and her bum when we came home. She would lift and turn her head away in disgust and embarrassment since this happened to be outside, next to our front door.

Since my office was on the main floor, she stayed with me. She would rest next to my desk, close to the radiator. At precisely 10:30 AM, she would put one paw on my knee. I would pretend not to notice. A minute later, she put both her front legs up and pushed her head through my arm, which rested on the desk. She was telling me to take a break and go out with her. She was quiet; she blended in – but she did not like the mailman. That was the only time she barked. She loved being in my car with me. She had a blanket on the back seat, but she would always sit up and watch where we were going. At one time, I came out of my bank and saw a lot of people standing around my car across the street. Alarmed, I crossed the road. Cindy was sitting in my seat with her paws on the steering wheel. Her eyes were on the door through which I had disappeared. When she saw me coming, she jumped back onto her blanket and took on an innocent air. She knew I did not like her to sit in front. The people told me that it was just too cute how the doggy pretended to be a driver.

I could tell endless stories about Cindy. It was a year later, and by now, Doris was also working in my skincare salon. After a busy day, I came home totally exhausted and just lay down on the blue carpet we had bought in Tunesia. Cindy was next to me, looking at me with understanding eyes. If I turned around, she walked around me and lay beside me, always with eye contact. Then the girls came home. They stood over me and declared:

"Mom, we have been thinking. You ought to raise our pay for each of us to a thousand dollars a month, or we will give notice. Coming from Giselle's, other shop owners know we are well trained, and we would even bring them the customers who always book with us."

It felt like a kick in the stomach. I already paid my daughters more than aestheticians usually got paid. They lived free at home and could save every penny. I was lying on the floor in pain, looking up at them, towering over me. I couldn't believe that my girls could treat me like that. It was blatant blackmail. They knew I would not want them to go and work for others and take my customers with them. I managed to whisper,

"Okay."

When Louis came home, and I told him what had happened, he was furious with me. That is an understatement. He accused me of spoiling them by always giving in. I should have let them go and find work somewhere else. A few months down the road, he suggested I open another salon since the girls could not get along working together. Reluctantly, I did precisely that. It was an 800

FLIGHT INTO THE UNKNOWN

square foot location next to 'Dirndl Stube,' a German dirndl dress & import shop, a hairdresser, a diner and a stereo shop and not far from the downtown Eaton's department store. My grand opening was a splash, attended by the Labour Minister of Manitoba, the German Consul, a German Newspaper journalist, and several other dignitaries, along with a radio station broadcasting on location. Doris became the manager, and I hired two other aestheticians. I overlooked that the inventories always showed shrinkage. I just didn't have the nerves anymore to be more involved or get upset. I said to myself, 'it's the price of being in business.'

My friend Walter, Gela's husband, told me about Gimli, an Icelandic town about a hundred kilometres away. He was involved in renovating former military housing into condos. He had bought one of those condos, and he convinced me to buy one as well. He thought them a profitable rental investment. They cost only $14,000. I saw mine as an occasional escape and paid for it from the business account. I could do my bookkeeping there and write my magazine articles in peace. I still had my old German travel typewriter. Perfect! I went furniture shopping with Eric. He promised not to tell anyone anything about our secret place. We furnished the two bedrooms and the living room. The kitchen was built-in; all I needed were dishes, glasses, cutlery and some pots and pans. My pride and joy was a large mural of a park with lots of bright-red tulips on one wall. The scene reminded me of the park surrounding the casino in Baden-Baden. Here, I could dream.

When Christmas came, I told my family we had an invitation to stay in Gimli. Once there, I admitted proudly that this was our place. Louis was jealous and couldn't be happy or enjoy himself, but I tried to be aloof and not notice it. He invested all his money in collecting stamps. Whenever I suggested any improvements to our house, he always told me, "I have no money, if you want that, pay for it." Since there was no television, the girls were bored after the initial excitement with the Christmas presents. Since Eric was a bookworm, he didn't mind. After two nights, we decided to go home again.

Another year went by, and I thought more earnestly about selling my retail business. In a few more months, my lease on Academy Road would be up. Did I want to commit to another five years above the 7-Eleven? My heart was giving me trouble again, I felt stressed, and my back always hurt. It was time to book my now annual Jamaica trip. So, after the year-end work, in January 1981, I left for two weeks of life in paradise.

I knew a few Jamaican people by now and looked forward to seeing them again. I registered with the Jamaican Tourist Office for the chance to be invited to private homes. I filled out a form and answered questions about my interests as 'medicine' and 'art.' The first week I was at a party in a doctor's house, during the second week, I attended an Art Gallery opening. I fell in love with a large painting, and it was hard not to buy it. The Jamaicans paint in vivid colours; I loved the happy topics, flowers, people, and landscapes. I was realistic: what was fitting for Jamaica wouldn't look right in Winnipeg.

One morning, I almost drowned during my swim. Something was sucking on the skin of my back, I tried to get it off by splashing around, but it didn't work. I frantically turned around and around, trying to reach for it, but nothing helped. I hurried back to the small beach where I could get in and out of the water. Several old fishers were sitting there fixing their nets. They looked at me, and one commented,

"You were in trouble out there. We almost came to rescue you. What was it?"

I told them about the sucking on my back and how I didn't know how to stop it.

"Lady, it's your bathing suit. It attracted sucker-fish, tiny fish who suck onto bigger ones to clean them. They took you for a large fish because of the colour of your bathing suit. They are quite harmless."

Harmless, eh? How could I have known that? My bathing suit was the colour of a spotted leopard. I never wore it for swimming again. It became my sauna suit. In Canada, we did not sauna in the nude like in Europe.

I had brought a bright, colourful one for walking or suntanning. It was now my swimsuit, and I bought a tiny bikini for suntanning.

'Jamaica – No Problem!'

FLIGHT INTO THE UNKNOWN

28: WHEN YOU DREAM - DREAM BIG

Worn out and depressed, I had gone to Jamaica. I came back with lots of energy and knew what I wanted to do. Before I'd left, I had seen a 'For Rent' sign on a beautiful commercial 2-storey building called 'Galleria,' a superb location with a floor to ceiling glass front. It was large, close to 3.000 square feet. I dreamed about it in Jamaica. I made plans for a layout in my head and on paper napkins. Coming home, I signed a lease for five years and handed in the notice for my present location on Academy. There were only three months left.

Heinz, a friend, working as a display designer for The Bay, was as excited as I was when I showed him the place. We went over my designs, and he had lots of ideas to improve them. Once I was satisfied, I called on another friend, Walter. His company arranged to build walls and dividers and did all the painting. I ordered the required equipment for the treatment rooms, shelving for the new health food section, products that fit my passion for skincare from within and without, an upright commercial display cooler with glass doors, a washer, dryer and more. The combination, skincare and health-food, was unique in North America. A large neon sign with the name 'Giselle's Professional Skin Care' was ordered and installed in the center of the three-part front window. It lit up automatically with the fading light. Slowly, my dream took shape, with many tradespeople working to meet my deadline. I hired a seamstress to sew cornflower-blue smocks that our customers could change into when having facials, massages, or waxing. Towels, sheets, and other items needed for the different treatments were on shelves in the utility room, which housed a double sink and the washer and dryer. I ordered three-quarter-length double-breasted white smocks with a half-belt in the back for all my employees. I wanted a professional look: no jeans, no slippers, no sneakers, but dark-blue dress pants or skirt and shoes with soft soles. This place was to be a quiet oasis for our customers with hardly noticeable soft classical music throughout.

I am a perfectionist. Everything had to be 'purrfect' - such as the world, especially my hometown, Winnipeg, had never seen: elegant, beautiful, functional, and for first-time visitors even awe-inspiring. And it was. When finished, I frequently asked myself: Was it really me who created this?

The square-footage was divided in length about 2/3 for the skincare area. I had planned 1/3 for reception/sales/health-food, and my office with a narrow one-way window, overlooking the reception area and the sales counter. I could see out, but nobody could see me. I always knew when there was a problem, and, casually, I would come out to solve it.

I loved my new wastebasket. A picture of a snoozing cat and a lion was on it, and a caption read,

'When you dream, dream big!'

My office door was always open. I encouraged my employees to come to me with a question or a complaint. Two leather chairs with a covered safe for a table were along one wall, facing this were three desks, one for the manager, one for the bookkeeper, and one for my secretary. Behind the dividing wall were a storage room, the packing and shipping area for mail order, my wholesale business and a small lunch station. Restrooms were close to the rear exit.

Clients entered through a glass front door. The sales counter and health food section were to the left. Turning right brought you into the elegant waiting room with a Persian rug and two beautiful dark-blue couches with a large pink flower design. Soft green chairs provided a counter-point. Fresh flowers and a fancy bowl with wrapped candies and chocolates were on the glass table in the centre. Customers could wait comfortably for any skincare treatments, manicures, pedicures, massages, waxing, make-up, the only tanning bed, or while waiting for their nails to dry. This room became like a club chatting room, especially on Thursdays and Fridays, for people who had standing manicure appointments and to hear the latest gossip.

Along one wall was a display of books with titles relating to healthy living. Eight manicure stations were placed along the large front window and the adjacent wall. A wall with built-in shelves, displays and mirrors was the make-up area, dividing the front room from the skincare section, and in the centre was the curtained entrance to the sanctum.

After changing into their blue smocks, clients went into one of the twelve numbered treatment rooms. Six cabins were on each side. At the end of the hallway, I had placed an oversized mirror with the words: 'You Are Beautiful,' etched in large, fancy letters. I noticed that many customers raised their heads and squared their shoulders when walking towards the mirror.

Behind that mirror, to the right, was the pedicure section with four modern off-white pedicure chairs. It was the only room where people could talk with each other – other than the waiting area. A wall divided this room from the utility area with hot and cold water and a door to the restrooms.

What became my flagship salon was what I had dreamed it to be: perfect, beautiful, elegant, and out of this world. After we finished everything, we placed 100 balloons on the ceiling. It was quite a job to blow them up. No machine… hahaha! With 250 embossed invitations, I invited Winnipeg's upper crust; politicians, Consular people, the media, newspapers, television, and radio to my Grand Opening and advertised the occasion everywhere. More people attended, according to the guest book. Eric was in charge of it, greeting people as they came in. He was sixteen, looking dapper in a suit, white shirt and tie. We made a huge splash. All the desks were full of flower arrangements and congratulatory cards; the shop was packed with beautifully dressed and smiling people, former and future clients. My family and my employees, which now numbered fifteen, wore beautiful corsages with pink carnations. They had a chance to mingle, offering finger-food and refreshments.

Within a year, my staff grew to eighteen. New employees did not have the training I desired, and I spent evenings and weekends to get them up to speed. If I paid them above minimum wage for three months and then hired them full-time, the government would refund the difference as a training allowance, so I did. Our Labour Minister mentioned that I was the only one in Manitoba who took advantage of this program. In July 1982, we were voted Best Skin Care Center in North America by a women's magazine.

The Galleria was very close to an intersection. Drivers, when stopped at the light, looked into our picture window at the girls sitting at the small white tables doing manicures. Once, we had a hilarious visit from two police officers. They had smiled, and waved, then found a parking spot and came in. They had mistaken us for an ice cream parlour!

People came for treatments from Minneapolis, Toronto, and even Montreal. They encouraged me to open salons in their cities, saying, "If you can make it in Winnipeg, you can make it anywhere." Giselle's was known all over Canada since I was still interviewed by radio and television across the country. I remember a musician from a band in Montreal. He suffered from a bad case of acne, and he hoped to find help at 'Giselle's.' In combination with our acne program, I used our tanning bed for medical reasons to treat cases like his. It was the time when people had started to eat less red meat and more chicken. He listened to my recommendations. It was interesting for me to follow his transformation. Young people who ate more chicken suffered from fewer acne problems since the food the chickens received was already treated with the same antibiotic (Tetracycline) doctors prescribed for bad acne cases.

Ella from Russia, who had been a doctor specializing in internal medicine, applied for a job. She had taken aesthetics in St. Petersburg because she knew her doctorate would not be recognized in Canada. Her English was weak. She had worked for Just Nails Ltd. for three weeks, but they let her go. She and her husband were recent immigrants. His parents had lived in Winnipeg for years. He was a neurologist but had to go back to university to be able to work in his field. Ella told me that one of them had to earn money. She had taken aesthetician training before leaving St. Petersburg and needed a job. I hired her and trained her on weekends. Oh, she was funny; she could never learn to pronounce the word sheet. She would call out,

"Giselle, where is the shit?"

FLIGHT INTO THE UNKNOWN

I would smile and quietly correct her, "Ella, it's "s h e e t !"
"Yes, Giselle, that's what I said..."

Or, she would come to my office to tell me with a stern expression about a problem she encountered.

"...and, Giselle, that's worser!"

For fun, we all adopted that one. Ella remained faithful to my business and became one of my most valuable employees.

My company was growing. I had a couple of requests to sell franchises. I was not too keen on it and talked to my lawyer. He advised it was time to change my provincial registration as a limited company to federal. I agreed with him for two reasons. First, it is advantageous to have a federally registered, limited company. Secondly, now nobody could go ahead and use my business name in another province – unless it was a franchise.

My husband wanted to be on my board of directors and become a 50% owner. I remembered when I, unpaid, had worked my butt off for Aetna Photo Laboratories, and how my money had given him the chance to start it. When things were not going well, he had installed a manager and went on holiday to Europe. I had no say in anything this manager did, spending money needlessly and running us towards bankruptcy. And now, Louis wanted to have 50% ownership and a voice in MY business? He had never helped me in the beginning when I packed dozens of small mail-order parcels after dinner when the children were in bed. When I worked seven days a week, often 'till after midnight? I offered him 49%; he said no, 50% or nothing. While we were sitting in the lawyer's waiting room, he said again:

"So? What is it? Do I get 50%?"

I felt my hair rise, but I told him, no, it's 49/51%. He got up, looked down at me, and requested in a stern voice,

"Giselle. It is 50% or nothing."

My scalp prickled, my stomach quivered, my heart raced. I quietly answered,

"Then, it's nothing."

Without a further word, he walked out. I registered the company with only three people on the board. He was not one of them. He avoided talking about my business, and he never offered any help when I needed it. However, he still came for his vitamins, for pedicures and the tanning bed, everything free of charge, naturally.

With all of the stress, I developed asthma. I had terrible dreams and couldn't breathe. Some attacks at night were so bad that Louis had to wake me. I ended up in the emergency room. The doctor referred me to a heart specialist. It took six weeks until I saw this Irishman, red hair and freckles, but full of humour and incredibly friendly. He did every test and, when he had done everything he could, he told me,

"Giselle, you surely have asthma. But there is no real reason for it, your heart and your lungs are okay. Would you mind if I send you to a psychiatrist?"

It confirmed my own diagnosis. I knew it was all from daily emotional stress. Why did I always feel better when I was away from home?

"If you think it will help me? Sure, go ahead."

He referred me to one of the leading psychiatrists of Winnipeg. It was a surprise; I knew this doctor through our social network. I had met him and his wife a couple of times at home parties. I decided not to tell him anything about my relationship problems. Men are always on the men's side - so how can I trust a man, especially a man who knew my charming husband? He prescribed some pills. I took one; it made me violently sick. I never took another. He explained that I would get used to the pills since they would change my brain waves. I told him I don't want anything to change my brain waves. He wasn't happy but insisted that I should continue to see him twice a week. After the third week, he knew everything. I remember the way he looked at me, leaned back in his chair and earnestly told me:

"If you don't want to die an early death, you must separate."

It wasn't a shock, I knew it. My reaction was,

"I don't want to do that. You confirmed my feelings. I'll make a greater effort to live with it."

The doctor was quite serious. "You need help. You need to be able to talk about it without fear and anxiety. At least keep your appointments with me. In the long run, I can help you."

"No, doctor, I'll not take up a place that somebody else might need more than I do. Maybe, if I can call on you if I get to the end of my rope…"

FLIGHT INTO THE UNKNOWN

"That might not be possible unless you jump through all the hoops again and get another referral. But I wish you good luck."

During the following months, I started to lose a lot of weight. I was getting my period not once a month, but every other week. I was afraid to see my doctor. Could it be cancer? But I took more vitamins, hoping it would help my immune system.

That summer, Bella spent her holidays in Vancouver. She came back happy, and she didn't stop talking about her birth city. The weather and the beaches were beautiful, and life was so different than in Winnipeg. I had a premonition that she would probably move. She did. She packed the Volkswagen she had bought from my business for book value and off she went. She told me her dream was to have her own business there. A hairdresser had offered her a back room. I spent $5,000 to set her up, got her all the needed equipment, and supplied the skincare products through my wholesale business.

Doris also had big plans. She wanted to take a year off and go travelling in Europe. I was worried about her, but she was a feisty, self-assured young lady, and she had a way of convincing us she would be safe. I never had a chance to take her to Jamaica. She returned from Europe almost a year later. She had met Nick, who became her husband. He wanted to immigrate to Canada, and the best reason for him to gain acceptance was to marry her within three months. We offered them a living space in our house. They would have a living room, a bedroom, a bathroom, and a kitchen for a token sum of $120 a month. My business paid $800 for the whole apartment but only used two rooms for my office; the rest was empty. Doris felt this sum was exorbitant. So they found another suite and paid more.

Eric decided to leave Ravenscourt School. He didn't like it, wanted to go to Kelvin High School, less than a block away, where all his buddies were. He took an extra-curricular law class. Since several of his forebears on his father's side were lawyers, we hoped he would study law. After the first term, he gave it up. We were disappointed and asked him why.

"All lawyers are liars. Have to defend a criminal or a murderer and get him off to prove how good a lawyer I am? I don't want to be that way."

Wearing a white lab coat, he worked in the health food section at Giselle's after school. He took an interest in health food products and studied many books about it. One, 'Life Extension,' became his Bible. It was brand-new. I had bought it at a health convention in Las Vegas. One day, a doctor came into the shop and asked me if I could get him that book. He had heard about it, but it was not yet available in Canada. He was an MD but was laid off from the military and wanted to get into the alternative health field. Naturally, I ordered the book for him. When he came back to pick it up, he gave me a typical doctor's look and asked,

"Are you alright? "

I knew I was pale, very thin, my weight was down to 98 pounds, and I had dark circles under my eyes.

It was a split decision. I told this stranger that I had lost a lot of blood because of my period being so frequent.

"What kind of vitamins do you take, do you have them here? I can do kinesiology testing. You may be taking something that isn't right for you."

I picked up the bottles of vitamins I was taking from my health food section, and he proceeded to test each one. I had to hold a bottle in my outstretched hand, he tried to push my arm down, and I was to resist as powerfully as I can. If he was able to get my arm down, he put that particular item aside. This exercise determined that I was allergic to vitamin E and the high dose of B complex I was taking.

"Please, stop taking these. Do you have any of your treatment rooms available? I would like to do some energy channelling for you."

I wasn't familiar with it, and he noticed that I hesitated.

"Don't worry. You don't have to undress, and I won't touch you."

One of my massage rooms was available. I had to lie down, relax and close my eyes. After a little while, I peeked, because I didn't notice anything. His hands were moving about eight or ten inches above me; his face was a study in concentration. I just closed my eyes again and thought, "what nonsense. Well, if it doesn't help, it doesn't hurt."

Somehow Dr. Owen Schwartz, this former military doctor, later famously infamous in Winnipeg, saved my life. Whatever he did, it worked, even if I didn't believe in it. After following his advice, I started to have regular menses again and also put on a bit more weight. A year down the road, he disappeared from Winnipeg. Eight patients had reported him, and he was losing his MD licence and was not allowed to practise. Fifteen hundred people demonstrated at City Hall, but it didn't help. I tried for several years to find him. Unsuccessfully. (long before Google!)

The New Year's party 1981/82 was at Gela and Walter's house in their spacious downstairs party room. The whole German gang was there, including us. As was typical, at the stroke of midnight, everybody was screaming and yelling and kissing everybody. I never liked this kissing tradition and left to go outside. It was a bright, frosty Winnipeg night, the sky full of tiny stars. I stood out there, shivering in my evening gown. I looked at the sky and prayed that all our problems would go away. When I thought the kissing was over, I returned - but, halfway down the stairs, I stopped and stared. The lady, I had envisioned a long time ago as Louis' third wife, sat on his lap, one hand on unmentionable parts of him. They were French-kissing, tongues in and out, they were really into it. Louis saw me standing on the stairs; he just lifted and dropped his shoulders and went on with it, despite all the people surrounding them.

I left and went to sit upstairs in one of the living room chairs in the dark. I felt so empty. My whole life flashed before my eyes. After a while, Gela came to sit with me. She told me I should not take this kissing too seriously, that lady is one of the so-called 'kissing gang,' and she does it with everybody. Gela tried to help me by telling some other stories she had witnessed, but it was as if her words were water, they flowed off me. If I had been a balloon, I'd know now what it's like to be deflated.

FLIGHT INTO THE UNKNOWN

29: PROBLEMS AND APOLOGIES

Louis apologized profusely for what I had seen at the New Years' party. It just happened; it didn't mean anything; they both were already more than a bit tipsy. He couldn't convince me that it was the whole story. I lived with it, but I could not forgive him. I slept in the smallest room on the third floor of our house; I stayed in my office until very late and never came down in the morning until I knew Louis had left for work. Life went on, I worked, I made dinner, and I kept the household functioning. I was a ghost in my own house.

My poodle, Cindy, had been run over in March. The road was icy. A couple of elderly ladies couldn't stop when Cindy suddenly ran in front of their large car, trying to get to another dog on the other side of the road. Their vehicle became a sled, Cindy was caught under one wheel and pushed along until they finally came to a stop. Her fur on one side was gone. Eric saw it happen. The ladies were upset, they cried, and offered to drive them to a veterinarian. From there, Eric phoned me, holding Cindy, wrapped in a towel, on his lap. When I entered, Cindy lifted her little head, looked at me with sorrowful eyes as if to say, "I'm so very sorry." I cried. A customer with a cat came in, and it was the last time she gave a sign that she was still alive. The doctor took her into his operating room, but he returned after not even a minute. He told us,

"She's gone. Do you want to take her body for burial, or do you want us to take care of it?"

"It's best you take care of it, doctor. The ground is still frozen. Thank you."

Eric and I were devastated. We cried and cried. Eric wrote a little poem. I do not have it anymore. It inspired me to write one as well:

> "Take More Time"
> Just sitting there.
> With big brown eyes, you looked at me
> To tell me – you are mine.
> And I pretend not seeing you
> because
> There was no time.
> Because there was no time?
> You loved the car. You want to come?
> One step – you stopped, then ran
> You couldn't resist to be with me
> One nod was all, oh, man!
> When I lay down – you did that too;
> You were so close to me.
> Oh, little dog, where are you now?
> I want you here, you see?
> I want you here, just sitting there.
> I'll tell you, you are mine.
> I love you unconditionally
> As you did all the time.
> It is too late. The car hit hard,
> Your eyes, they closed forever.
> I'll never see your wagging tail
> Invite for play me, clever.
> It will be quiet at my house
> No welcome bark nor whine.
> Oh, Cindy, why, oh, Cindy why
> Did I not take more time!
> Did I not take more time…

I cried for six weeks. Then Eric took charge.

"Mom, we have to get a new dog. I found one in the paper. Look, here:

FLIGHT INTO THE UNKNOWN

'Silver-grey poodle needs a loving home. $100. Phone…'

It belonged to a dog trainer. He also had a German shepherd. He proudly showed us how well trained the dogs were and put some food into the doggie bowl. The shepherd got his nose right into it and pushed the poodle away. With a stern voice, the man commanded,

"Ajax! Apologize to Pepper!"

The big dog went and briefly licked Pepper's little face, and both dogs proceeded to feed out of the same bowl. We were suitably impressed and bought Pepper.

After a few days, we noticed Pepper was limping. We took him to a vet. He just took one look and exclaimed,

"I know this dog! An abusive dog trainer kicked him down the stairs. I operated on him; he has a silver hip. There isn't much I can do right now, but give Pepper some rest, don't walk him too much right now."

Sadly, my relationship with Pepper was not what I had with Cindy. He hated to be left alone. To punish me, he would put droppings on my Persian rugs. Since the carpets were so colourful, one could not see the poop until one stepped into it. Stephany, my cleaning woman, told me she would quit. Either the poodle goes, or she goes. Since I couldn't take him with me to my business due to health laws, I had no choice. My bookkeeper Alice took him, and he was happy there. Her husband was at home doing renovations. Their two boys were crazy about him. I visited three years later, and I couldn't believe that Pepper still remembered me. He jumped onto my lap, cuddled, and was excited to see me. Alice sat across from me and quietly said,

"My goodness, I can't believe it. I thought he was totally our dog and forgot you."

Pepper heard that, jumped down, up onto her lap, and proved how much he loved her, practically washing her face. I was happy to see that he had a better home than we had been able to provide for him

Later in spring 1982, I was on a car trip through Western Canada. Just before Field, B.C., I drove up a mountain on a logging road. I wanted to turn around somewhere and, on the way down, go over the edge. I saw a perfect spot. When the moment came, I thought of my son and couldn't do it.

My next appointment was in Kelowna. There, somebody stole my purse out of my car. I had run into a store to drop off a handful of flyers, leaving the passenger side window open. An envelope with about $250.00 cash and cheques amounting to almost a thousand dollars was in my purse. My driver's licence gone; I had to deal with the police. I then had to cancel my credit cards and inform the shop-owners who had issued those cheques.

In the evening, I went swimming in the lake by the motel. I swam far out to get tired and somehow anticipated I might not make it back. A father and daughter, visiting from Victoria, had been watching me from their balcony. They came to help in a small boat and ended up becoming good friends. Once again, I did not succeed in killing myself.

It was during July of 1982 that Belinda, one of my regular customers, asked me,

"Giselle, have you ever thought of selling your business?"

Of course, I had thought of it but had never mentioned it to anyone. I loved my new shop. I had also never told anyone how my husband kept pushing me to move out. I had asked him, 'why me, why not you?' His answer was, 'whoever has the best nerves and stays will get the house. That's surely not you.'

I looked at Belinda, who was getting a manicure and answered, "No, I haven't."

"Then start thinking about it. I am interested. I want to buy it."

I nodded at her. A few days later, her mother came in for a manicure. She was a regular customer; she lived in a gorgeous old house in our neighbourhood. She knew about her daughter's ambition and warned me,

"Giselle, be careful. My daughter looks like an angel, but she is a devil."

Wow, I didn't expect that to hear from a mother. She was serious - I laughed.

Louis had a heart attack; the doctors called it a warning. He was in the hospital for ten days, four in intensive care. My mother was in the hospital in East Germany. My father was distraught, afraid she would die. He sent a telegram asking if I could come to see her again before it was too late. I had an anxiety attack caused by the stress, and ended up back in the emergency room myself,

FLIGHT INTO THE UNKNOWN

shortly after Louis returned home. Luckily, a few weeks later, I was able to fly to Germany. Mom did not look good.

Father and I spent every day with her in the hospital. He was devastated. He told me,

"It's so quiet and empty at home. She complained a lot, but at least she was there, and I was not alone. I don't know what I'll do if she dies. I can't even cook an egg."

They had been married for fifty years. We were relieved when Mom recovered. I had to leave a week later and hoped for the best. My youngest sister Edith and her family lived less than an hour away. Dad had bought a car for them, so they were able to check on our parents occasionally. The trouble was, nobody had a telephone. Edith wrote me an unfriendly letter accusing me and Christel, our other sister, of burdening her with looking after our elderly parents after we escaped to the west. She felt it was unfair that we were not around to help. I wrote back and explained that we had escaped almost thirty years ago when she was ten years old, and our parents were around fifty, young enough and healthy. At that time, none of us had thought of who would look after them in their old age.

At the end of July, I attended the American Health Convention in New Orleans. I was shocked to find a four-page letter from Louis in my suitcase. He complained about having to spend so much time alone since I was working up to 18 hours a day, and we didn't have parties in our house anymore since I am always away. He also complained that he didn't even know anymore what sex was. He still loved me, but something would have to change. A lovely letter – but why had he kept pushing me to move out? Had his heart attack changed his thinking?

A group of conventioneers took me under their wing. Jazz was heard everywhere, often out of open windows, as we experienced New Orleans nightlife. We visited a few live jazz venues and listened to fabulous music. One place had a slanted mirror all along above the stage where two piano players battled with each other. In that mirror, I could see us sitting together like birds on a wire. A pair of large grey eyes caught mine. It was one of those moments when you just know something is going to happen. The eyes belonged to Richard; he was one of our group. The next morning, he was with several other people. He spotted me coming out of the elevator and asked me to join them for breakfast at 'Café Du Monde,' a famous New Orleans Café. I did. After breakfast, he showed me a two-inch gold-dipped seahorse pendant.

"I bought this at Pike Place Market the last time I was in Seattle. It is a real seahorse, and I liked it. Would you wear it on your necklace if I gave it to you? I have nobody to give it to; it's a lucky charm."

"Richard, I'm a stranger, why would you want to give me that? Funny that it is a seahorse, I have always liked watching them in the Vancouver Aquarium."

He explained that he wanted to pass it on; it seemed to matter to him. I did not have the heart to turn him down and accepted it. Walking back to the Convention Center, we had to stop for traffic. He grabbed my hand to cross the street. I pulled it away from him after we crossed. He grinned while looking at me.

"You don't like holding hands, do you?"

In August, my husband went on holiday to Cuba. Years later, I learned that his New Year's kissing partner was there as well. A week after Louis had left, Richard called me. We had a friendly chat on the phone. Eric and I were alone. Richard invited me to join him and a few friends, going to Alaska for five days. I could not commit to it; I had to wait until Louis was back as I didn't want to leave Eric alone. When I finished the call, Eric looked at me with wide-open eyes.

"Mom. Your aura was glowing white! It was scary. Don't hurt that man."

I did go. The Alaska trip put my life on a different path. I had never been unfaithful, but it happened in Alaska at the 'Grande Denali Lodge.' During our lovemaking, if I could call it that this first time, Richard breathed hard and uttered,

"You – are – killing – me."

I was rather passive as I was kind of studying him and answered,

"You? You are killing yourself – and me in the process."

He laughed, and all the tension was gone. We had a quiet conversation about my life – and his life. I told him,

"I don't believe that you don't have a woman in your life. You know how to treat a woman. Will you tell me about her?"

FLIGHT INTO THE UNKNOWN

He circumvented the question. He told me about one snowy night meeting someone when he went on a walk. "Ships, passing in the night," he said. "Sure, occasionally, there is one, but it never lasts. I don't have someone I deeply love."

"Why did you invite me to come to Alaska with you?"

"I don't know. Maybe to get to know you better?" And that was the end of it.

Have I ever been in love? Really in love? Thinking back, it was always more a conscious decision to love or like (?) someone – this was different. I felt as if I had known Richard all my life. There was a deep inner connection. If this man had said, "let's die together," I would have been willing. No, not right now; those feelings came later, years later.

FLIGHT INTO THE UNKNOWN

30: A BOUNCED CHEQUE

In October, I went to the annual Canadian Health Food Industry Convention in Toronto. I was one of the speakers and had also rented an exhibition booth. I displayed my skincare products, did demos, and took orders. I left Winnipeg late afternoon on a Thursday with one of my aestheticians and returned on Monday morning.

I found a bounced cheque on my desk for $53.90. I had written it to pay for the replacement of a caster on one of the kitchen chairs. I had an excellent credit rating and was more than upset, afraid I might lose it because of such a stupid mistake. It must be a mistake, as we had our joint private checking and saving accounts as well as my business account at that bank, with plenty of money to cover it. I was angry. I called my bank manager; we had a good relationship.

"Barbara, I can't believe you let a small cheque bounce on me. You know there is enough money to cover it in that account. Even if there weren't, your bank could have covered it. How can this happen, who made a mistake? Did they not check with you? You know, I don't want to lose my credit rating with Dunn & Bradstreet..."

"Giselle, simmer down. Please come to my office as soon as you can. I am sorry, but I have to give you some bad news. Not over the phone. I am free right now."

Steaming with rage, I jumped into my car and raced off. Luckily, I didn't receive another speeding ticket. I had three already. At five, I would lose my driver's licence.

Barbara was waiting for me in her office. She urged me to sit down, take a deep breath and listen to what she had to say.

"Giselle, your husband came to us on Friday morning and closed all the accounts. I tried to stop him. He didn't give me a reason, just insisted on transferring it all to his bank. Not just the joint checking and savings account, also the total of $28.000 in your rental house account, and all the money from your business checking account. It all amounted to about $100,000. I'm sorry to tell you, but you don't have a single penny left. He also insisted we call a locksmith to open your safety deposit box because he misplaced the key. I had a terrible feeling about his behaviour and held him off by saying we need three days' notice for such a request. That worked. I prayed that you would be back in time. Sorry, dear, but there you have it. What you do next is up to you. It was a big mistake to let him have signature rights to all your accounts. At least I saved you the contents of your safety deposit box."

I fainted. Barbara jumped up, opened her door, and yelled for someone to bring cold water quickly. They put a cold cloth on my forehead and tried to give me some water to drink. I lay there, wondering if I would suffer a heart attack. My chest exploded with pain. I heard them debating if they should call an ambulance. I recovered sufficiently and whispered,

"No. No, I don't want an ambulance. They would bring me to the hospital and call my husband, and he is the last person I want to see right now."

Barbara did not let me leave for another hour as she felt it wasn't safe for me to drive. I realized my life had changed within the last few minutes. I would have to make a decision. I would have to find the strength to have a conversation with Louis. After all, he wanted the house and everything in it, including that damned kitchen chair. Tomorrow, I would have to phone my lawyer and ask him how to handle this.

That night, I stayed with my friend Marianne whom I knew since Eric was a baby. I cried my heart out and told her everything. She remained calm, bent over her knitting, and then stated a fact.

FLIGHT INTO THE UNKNOWN

"Move out. You can stay with me until you find an apartment. I know you can't stand up to Louis. Talk to your lawyer. I am sorry, my friend, but I think you are heading for a divorce."

That brought on more tears. The next morning, the lawyer advised me to take any of my valuables, even my mink coat and the ermine jacket, to my business. He was glad I had already changed the name on the now-empty accounts. He also advised me to empty the safety deposit box and change the locks to my business doors.

So what do I do now?

After visiting the lawyer, I went home. I felt sick, but life goes on, and I had to face what was coming next. Louis was still at work, and I had the house to myself. Sitting at my large Jacobean antique desk, I looked around the living room. There was the impressive matching Jacobean breakfront cabinet, part of the complete set I had bought at an antique auction. It was taken apart into three sections but was still too large to come in through our front door. I had to hire a company to hoist it through one of the large veranda windows on the second floor. The set originated from a Hungarian castle; it was made in the late 19th century. It suited our old mansion.

I loved antiques and had collected many pieces. One of my favourites was a beautiful old painting of an ornamental brass pot with a colourful flower arrangement on a black background in the baroque style. Louis hated it. I had it framed in a heavy gold frame that was costlier than the painting. I had not been allowed to hang it in the living room; it was in our bedroom behind the door. There was also the Turkish throne with hand-carved half-moon motives. It had been my gift to Louis one Christmas. In the centre of the room was the six-piece modern Welby's sectional sofa set I had bought just months ago. We still had the mid-century Telefunken stereo console I had brought with me from Germany in 1963.

To the left and the right of my desk were two deep pink antique wing chairs, still built on springs. And, towards the far end of the room was a gorgeous 19th-century walnut chest. That's not counting the oversized modern painting over the sectional and the large portrait of Granny as a six-year-old child, a pastel done by her aunt. Two large lithographs with Berlin motives hung to my left. I had bought them for Louis as a birthday gift. A sizable Inuit sculpture was on top of the stereo console with an ancient painting of medieval soldiers above it. A 14x18-foot large soft-beige, thick Chinese rug covered parts of the floor plus the blue Turkish one, the one I would lie on with my frequent backaches.

When our consular friends transferred to Germany, I had bought several East Indian brass pieces from them. They were museum quality and quite valuable. I should undoubtedly take those with me; Louis had often called them junk. As I was sitting there, contemplating what, when, and how to make my next step, time flew by. I shook myself awake and started looking through boxes of photographs, all the ones that were not in albums yet. Louis had printed three and four of each to have copies for relatives. I sorted some that I thought would be nice for an album I could later leave for Eric. Looking through the photos, I remembered the cold February day in 1945 when I found all of my parent's photographs on our pile of manure when the Russians had invaded our village. Everybody had been ordered out of their homes with nowhere to go. What an awful time to remember that now.

My arms full of clothing, and a bag with my personal albums and the photographs, I finally went to my office. I just didn't have the heart to take anything else at this time. I thought it fair to speak to Louis first. Hindsight is 20/20.

I made sure that I was at home when he arrived. I had made dinner. We were both careful in what was said – we both avoided the issue, I guess, to spare our son. Louis must have realized that I knew about the bounced cheque and his emptying the accounts. After dinner, when Eric was upstairs in his room, I brought it up. Louis exploded. At the end of his tirade, he added,

"I hope you finally move out. And, take that junk with you," pointing to the Jacobean set. "I'll make sure you spend your old age in the poor house. You were lucky that you hid the key for the safety deposit box. I wanted to empty that too, but the bank didn't allow me to order a locksmith. You bought yourself a lot of jewelry, and I wanted to take it."

It was tough to remain quiet. How could my husband be so mean? I had always thought of him as an aristocratic gentleman. And I had wanted to be fair and had not taken anything, thought to talk to him first. I tried hard not to cry.

FLIGHT INTO THE UNKNOWN

"I did not hide the key. It is where it always was. Take a look. As for the jewelry, there were expensive pieces for you. I bought several items for the girls; and a necklace with a scorpion for Eric. It wasn't just for me. Look at your Swiss watch; look at your large 18-carat family ring with the carving of your family crest in the lapislazuli, and the 18-carat necklace with your astrological sign. Did you forget the diamond tie clip and several sets of gold cufflinks? The gold ring with the nine diamonds? How could you say that it was all for me? Didn't you realize I always spent much more money on gifts for you?"

I opened the right drawer of my desk. Louis looked and saw the safety deposit box key where it had always been, just behind the folder with all the letters he wrote to me while we were penfriends. That took the wind out of his sails for a few moments.

When Eric joined us, we stopped talking.

Within the next week, I finalized my plans to move out. Heinz, my friend from The Bay, was able to arrange the same company that had moved the Jacobean furniture in, to hoist it out again. While they were taking it apart, I sat on the floor and sorted through my books, most from Germany. After twenty years, I was still a member of a German book club and had to order one book each month. But we had dozens of Readers Digest condensed books. I divided them into two piles, one for him, one for me. In hindsight, how stupid! Why didn't I take first what was rightfully mine? All of a sudden, there was the voice of a ghost behind me. It creeped me out, made me shiver with fright, and I broke into a cold sweat.

"What are you doing? So you are finally moving out. Be aware that you will never get the house or any parts of the contents."

Louis had come home unexpectedly. How did he know? Did a neighbour phone him because of the moving truck? Did Eric? He watched my every move; it was unnerving. When I wanted to take my dark painting, the one he hated so much, he loudly commanded:

"That stays here. You can take the soldiers."

"But, Louis, you never liked it. That's why it's behind the door, and you always liked the soldiers. (originally, they were mine too) Why should I take those?"

"Because I say so. And those Indian brass pieces you bought from the Consul, they stay here as well. And the large amethyst rock on the side table."

"But…"

"Shut up. There are several other things you better not touch. Your Meissen collection, the Bohemian crystal glasses, the Persian rugs in your downstairs office. Yes, and all of the kitchen stuff."

I had made twelve pillows covered with Persian Maiden rugs for the beige sectional. Six of those pillows were missing. When I asked him, he said, "I hid them." The letters, the ones he had written to me in 1963 when we were penfriends, were gone too. And so were many others of my belongings, even items I had brought from Germany.

Most of my clothing was in two suitcases and my overseas trunk. I left four wigs with different hairdos on model heads, standing in my closet, my summer and beachwear, and other stuff I thought I could get later. I had taken only one soup pot and three knives, forks and spoons of the cutlery I had brought from Germany. Luckily, the stereo console and the suitcases were already in the moving truck. So was my Sarouk Persian rug from the den. Since I didn't have very much, it all fit into my office and the stockroom.

When I came back the next day to pick up the rest of my things, he had changed the locks to the house. When I asked Eric to get me my German beach bag and some summer clothing, he told me that his dad had forbidden him to get me anything of what I had left the day before. He denied having called his dad about the moving truck.

Despite everything, the thought of Louis' face when he opened my closet and saw the four wig-heads staring at him out of the emptiness, put a little smile on my lips.

My friend Marianne had offered me her small second bedroom. Hardly a night went by without me crying myself to sleep.

FLIGHT INTO THE UNKNOWN

31: SELLING THE BUSINESS

A day after the confrontation with Louis, I told Belinda that I was ready to talk. She did not seem surprised. I thought she might have changed her mind. I left it at that for now. Near the end of October, Belinda told me to take inventory with cost prices so that she can make an offer. Her proposal was $25,000 lower than the base cost of everything on the list. This amount was the cost of the equipment and product inventory of the downtown location. She did not want to pay for it, but she would take it anyway if I included it in her offer - unless I could sell it separately.

The health food section did not interest her either; the shelving could stay, but she suggested I advertise an exclusive sale of the products. I recommended the take-over for the 1st of January. She was adamant that we complete the transaction by the 1st of December. She wanted the pre-Christmas business. I told her, I counted on that too. In that case, there was no deal. Another condition was that I remain (unpaid) manager for the business since she had booked a holiday starting the 3rd of December. She wanted me to stay until she could run the business by herself. She did have a business degree but no aesthetic training.

One day I received an anonymous letter in the mail telling me that my two downtown employees were deceiving me. They had rented a small space in Eaton's Place to establish their own business while still being employed and paid by me. One would work there, while the other worked in my shop. If I dropped in unexpectedly, the one in my shop would tell me the other was out for coffee or lunch. I did not believe the anonymous writer. When I confronted the girls, I was shocked when they admitted to it. I might have been able to fire them on the spot, but I checked with the Labour Board. They advised me to let them work in my other shop for the two weeks that I had to give them notice. One of them agreed, and the other filed a claim through the labour board. It was a lot of extra stress, but she lost, the board decided I was within my rights and had been more than fair.

I offered the downtown location to my daughter Doris for a token fee of one dollar. I had helped Bella to start her own business in Vancouver, and I thought it fair to give Doris the established downtown Giselle's she knew well. She did not want it. I never attempted to sell it separately.

With the help of my lawyer, I completed the deal to sell my business. I included both locations in the offer and agreed to all Belinda's other conditions. She received the rights to my business name for the province of Manitoba. Work went on as usual; the sale was a relatively simple transaction.

Above my store, on the top floor of the Galleria, two windowless rooms were available. I rented those open-ended. Several friends helped me to move my office furniture and my wholesale stock up there. It was a practical solution. I could keep an eye on the 'Giselle's' business and keep my wholesale and mailorder running with my secretary. My bookkeeper would now only come once a month, and my accountant once a year.

Alone again

It was Eric who found a two-bedroom apartment for me. I moved in on November 15th, 1982. It was on Wellington Crescent, walking distance to my business. I felt sure it was for the two of us. An old doctor had lived there for many years, and I was able to buy some of his belongings. I hired movers to pick up the furniture from my Gimli condo. I had decided to rent it out. My new home was cozy, and when I asked Eric to bring his clothing and books, he surprised, no, actually shocked me.

"Mom, I am not moving in with you. I'll stay with Dad. This building is like an old folks' home, and I cannot play loud music here. And you don't really have any room for me in your life."

FLIGHT INTO THE UNKNOWN

Ouch! Did my boy know how much he hurt me? Stay with Dad? He had told me about the day he crawled under the kitchen table when his dad kicked him. I don't know why he did, but Louis had a choleric temper. Once, he had lifted his hand to hit me, and I had looked at him and growled, "just once, you hit me just once…" I had been abused this way in Germany and had promised myself, 'never again.' That was years ago. If he had hit me, it would have been the end of our marriage. Would it have been better? It would have saved me years of stress and agony, but I did not want to lose my family. My family was my base; I loved the children, had always felt responsible for their wellbeing. I felt grounded; I could fly out but always come back to my home base. Now, all that had changed.

The year 1982 came to a close. I would be alone for Christmas since Doris and Eric would spend it with their father. Bella lived in Vancouver. I confided in Richard, and he invited me to spend Christmas in Denver. I loved the 'Molly Brown Hotel,' admired all the old photos of Molly's life from rags to riches, and was stunned by the story of her surviving the Titanic disaster. 'The Unsinkable Molly Brown, wow!' I was delighted to find my room decorated with a small Christmas tree in a flowerpot, a stuffed Santa hanging in front of the window, and some other colourful decorations. Richard had left a note saying that he would stop by but was obligated to spend the holiday with his family. Yes, I had found out that he was married and had two teenage children. His wife was mentally challenged, but for financial and other reasons, he could not leave her - another soap opera.

Louis wanted my lawyer to handle both his and my separation to save money. He argued:

"Giselle and I agree. I get the house and all that's in it. I get the rental property because Aunt Anna told me so. I want the Mercedes and also the Sarouk rug. Yes, and I want the Gimli condo. And Giselle can keep her business."

My lawyer declined. "You need to hire your own lawyer. I cannot deal with both of you."

I brought up Louis's extensive stamp collection. Once, when a young niece of his had visited, he had told her that it was worth $476,000. She was in awe when she told me. When I asked him, he denied it. When my lawyer checked into it, he learned that 'collections do not have to be shared.' Louis even denied owning any stamps, which was an outright lie. They were in his friend's safe. What about my Meissen china collection? He kept that… Did the law not apply to me?

I had bought and paid monthly for life insurance in both our names. Louis did not believe in life insurance; he considered it a waste of money. He never contributed. In case something happened to us, I wanted to keep the children safe. A little over $3,000 had accumulated when I called the company. They told me I could stop paying. They would use the accrued money to deduct the monthly dues until we resolved our problems. Three years later, Louis received a letter from the company that money was running out. He cancelled it. The insurance company contacted me and offered me one-half of the remaining 300 dollars. Louis insisted I sign a form to let him have it all. My lawyer did not allow me to sign it.

"Enough is enough," he told me. "Even if 150 dollars is peanuts compared to what you let him get away with."

For Louis, it wasn't enough. He even had the gall to send me the bill for his lawyer. And no, he didn't get the Gimli condo nor the Mercedes as both belonged to the business. I never got the Liechtenstein stamp collection he had promised me when I paid for his Cadillac. I had sent a letter suggesting selling the Annaburg, give Bella and Doris their parts and put Eric's in trust until he grows up. I never received an answer from Aunt Anna. Louis claimed he did. He requested to transfer the rental property into his name, insisting she had demanded it. Why had I not asked to see proof or contact her myself again? I was either too proud or too burned out. I found it easier just to sign it over. I thought, "he is the children's father; he will not cheat them out of their inheritance and the gift from her." He did, not much later, when he sold it for double what I had paid, and gave each child only $1,000 each. Now, after approximately sixty years, and reading my diary of the time, I know he tricked poor Aunt Anna and me; what must she have thought of me, trust me, and then not even hear more from me about the whole disaster.

A Separation Agreement was drawn up by Louis' lawyer. Against the advice of my lawyer, I signed that, for a token of $1.00, I do not want anything. I never received the $1.00 either. If I

FLIGHT INTO THE UNKNOWN

had, I would have framed it. It would have served as a reminder of what twenty years of marriage were worth, raising his children and our son, and working myself to the bone. Looking at it would have reminded me never to trust so fully again.

.

FLIGHT INTO THE UNKNOWN

32: AN OTHERWORDLY EXPERIENCE

For my birthday in January 1983, Richard sent me a ticket to meet him in Hawaii. I was depressed, and I cried for most of the week we were there. He was patient and let me be. I heard more about his life, and I started to trust him, I could openly talk. Back in Winnipeg, I looked after the business, did my TV show and just 'existed' from day to day. Bella wrote from Vancouver:

"Mom, can you imagine? I had a letter from Kirsten. She stayed away from us because she could never have given us the upbringing you did, but now that you are gone, she would like to reconnect. Mom, she signed the letter with 'Your biological Mama.' That's all I needed! You are the only mother I ever knew. Why don't you move to Vancouver? Then I have you here, and Doris has Daddy there."

I had to stay a year to honour my contract with Belinda. In the salon, nothing much had changed. The health food section was now a lovely gift section. The shelving was gone, and several small round tables with floor-length tablecloth displayed a variety of pretty items.

Louis was horrible in his hate. I have no idea what kind of lies he told the children, but their behaviour was intolerable. Worse, I put up with it. I commented to my lawyer,

"How can Louis be so mean to me? Even ruining my relationship with the children?"

Straightening up in his chair, he said, "Well, wouldn't you be mad too if your best asset walked out the door?"

No, I could never be like that. Why didn't I fight for the house or my belongings he took? I was afraid of Louis. I was scared of his lawyer-father, who had talked me out of visiting Vancouver and meeting his son before I got married. I sacrificed my rights because I did not want to take the children's home base away, even if only Eric lived with his dad. They should not lose that. I did not want the Bader family and especially the children, to think bad of me. Doris shocked me one day:

"You don't run away from a marriage. You work at it."

My God, did she have any idea what had been going on? How hard I tried to accept the emotional abuse? No, she couldn't know, she didn't live with us. And I never talked about it.

It was dark when I woke up on April 7. I had the incredible feeling of floating over my bed. I had heard someone calling, "No, don't go, please no, no, no…" I felt for something reliable and was grateful when I touched my pillow. It was wet. I was flat on my back. I did not move and tried to shake the cobwebs off my mind. Who had been calling? Why would my pillow be wet? My hair on both sides of my face was soaked, and there was moisture in my ears too. I touched my eyes. Yes, I was crying, the tears kept running out of my eyes, and it seemed that a floodgate had opened. I couldn't stop it. I couldn't properly wake up, either. Weird, I knew I wasn't quite awake, I also knew I wasn't asleep. My dark bedroom felt cold and empty. Very empty. Almost hollow.

My alarm clock went off at 6.30 AM. A bit of grey light shone through the curtains. It took me a while to gather my thoughts. The wet pillow was a puzzle. I figured I must have had a bad dream and cried. Walking to the bathroom, I felt lightheaded and very sombre. I had my shower, dried myself, put my housecoat on, and padded back to the bedroom. I dressed without thinking. I chose everything black: a black pantyhose, black dress with a high collar, buttoned half-way down the front with small round shiny black buttons, black pumps. Back in the bathroom, I stared into the mirror: Why did I dress in black? I opened a drawer and pulled out my opera length white baroque pearls and hung them around my neck. I shook my head to the image in front of me and took them off again. I was very pale and had dark circles under my eyes.

Eventually, I set off to drive to my office. I sat in my car and prayed that my secretary would not notice my eyes, still red from crying. That sombre feeling had remained. As I entered through the back door, I pasted a smile on my face when I called out 'Good Morning' and hoped it sounded cheerful enough. June was at her desk, giving me a rather emotional look and saying somewhat timidly, 'Good Morning, Giselle.' I thought, what's with her? I put my coat behind my always-open office door. I sat down at my Jacobean desk in my Jacobean chair, folded my hands in my lap, and did absolutely nothing. I didn't see anything either. I was numb.

After maybe ten minutes, June called out, "Giselle, telephone for you." I picked it up and said my name.

"Hi, Giselle, it's Nick. I am afraid I have bad news for you."

"Yes, I know, my father died."

"Oh, you know already."

"Nick - no, I don't - what did you just say? How do you know?"

"Doris received a telegram for you this morning since she was the only person with the same last name on Grosvenor Avenue."

I was stunned. I hung up the phone and just sat there, my heart racing and my mind reeling. My hands were shaking; I couldn't stop them. I slowly started to understand my tears during the night, my sombre mood, my disconnection with reality. My father had written me a letter on February 17, complaining that he didn't feel well, that not even his cigars tasted good anymore. I had not heard from home since. Neither my mother nor my youngest sister had written to let me know that he was gravely ill. Today was April 7, 1983. There would have been time enough since February to let me know and give me a chance to fly home and see him again before it was too late. How good is it to attend the funeral of someone you love so much? Now, with no visa, no chance to even be there? Oceans were between us. They lived in East Germany, had tried to escape as I did, but my father had had a kidney attack on the way to the train station and ended up in the hospital. Despite my many warnings, they had waited for Edith to graduate. That was on August 11, 1961. Two days later, the Berlin Wall was up.

"June. Nick just told me my father died." I had left my office and stood in front of my secretary's desk.

"I am so very sorry, Giselle. I thought you knew."

"No, June, I did not know. It just hit me the moment Nick said it."

"But then, Giselle, why did you dress like that?"

"I have no idea. I wasn't aware of what I was doing. I thought I must have had a nightmare because I had cried so much last night, and my pillow was wet…"

I walked away from her towards the open area, the elegant waiting room with the manicure tables all around the glass windows. I stopped at every station to greet my customers and stood a bit longer at my daughter Doris' place. She lived with Nick. Her head was bent way down - I understood that she did not want to face me.

"Doris, Grandpa has died."

She never looked up from her work. "Yes, I know. You did too, didn't you?"

"I had no idea. Nick just called me a few minutes ago."

"But then - why did you dress like that?"

My back prickled, the hair at my neck was standing up as the full force of what happened last night hit me. My father had come to say 'Good Bye' - and the voice calling "No, don't go, please, no, no, no…" must have been my own.

The funeral was on April 9 – there was no way that I would be able to get a ticket, a visa and fly to Germany to attend. I wouldn't even arrive on time if I left today.

The soonest I could book my trip was August. My mother asked me to sleep in Dad's bed, next to hers. I couldn't. I slept on my childhood straw bed in the garden cottage. For breakfast, she placed me at Dad's usual seat in the sofa corner. I broke down and cried. She was annoyed and stated bitterly,

"You! What reason do you have to cry? You weren't here, and you didn't come for the funeral, you have no idea what I went through, seeing him die, choking to death. Listen to his last words, "I hope Gila is okay." No, you have no reason to cry."

She was hostile. I was hurt; I could hardly stand it. Neither my mother nor my sister Edith had let me know that he had lung cancer. Edith even accused me of killing him with his constant worries about me. I was glad to leave and fly back to Canada.

FLIGHT INTO THE UNKNOWN

33: AN AFFAIR WITH OMAR SHERIF?

We were sitting at Tubby's pizza restaurant on Stafford Street in Winnipeg, just around the corner from Giselle's. Jenny from CBC Radio had asked to meet me for lunch. She had already interviewed me several times. I admired her, she was smart, and a good interviewer. She joked,
"I know, I am not pretty, but I am good at what I do. They will never let me do TV interviews. If I had a choice to be either beautiful or intelligent, I would choose to be beautiful. Right now, I have to deal with being intelligent."
Intelligent she was. Doing radio work suited her. For me, it would have been a difficult decision. I thought, "I am glad to have both..." without saying it. Vain? Hmm. One of her next comments floored me:
"Giselle, tell me, how, when and where did you meet Omar Sharif? Is it true you two met in Las Vegas?"
Omar Sharif? How would I know Omar Sharif?! I didn't know Omar Sharif, and I told her so. She did not give up.
"Come on, Giselle, this affair of yours is a great news story; come on my program and let me interview you about it. And don't deny it - it's all over Winnipeg. I had it confirmed by a reliable source."
"But Jenny, it's not true! I only know him as an actor from the movie 'Dr. Zhivago' and the bridge section in the Winnipeg Free Press. Why would a famous man like him be interested in me? Besides, he is a heavy smoker and a well-known gambler, often

making a fortune and losing it again. Everything I know about him would not in the least fit my taste or my lifestyle."

I was trying to make light of it by telling her how I had cried when he, in the movie 'Doctor Zhivago,' collapsed and died of a heart attack on the sidewalk in Moscow. He was in a streetcar when he saw Lara, got out and was running after her. She never turned around, and he never caught up with her. I saw the movie with my eight-month-old baby boy on my lap who had been so good during the long hours. I couldn't convince Jenny. She expressed how she had thought I had more trust in her and was disappointed in me. I felt upset, and my voice was shaky.

"Jenny, I am telling you the truth. Who is your reliable source?" She would not reveal this information. Her parting words were,

"Why don't you phone him and then give me a call. Let me know if Sharif is okay with you telling the story."

A few days later, I walked, as I regularly did, through the store, greeting and exchanging a few words with the customers in every area: first at the manicure tables, then the facial and massage cabins and last the pedicure room with four chairs. Pedicures had become popular since I had taped a TV show showing a pedicure on a man. This show had brought a lot of new customers. Today, one of the ladies tried to keep me close by asking all kinds of questions relating to my frequent travels for lectures and health-related conventions. I did not know her, but I knew of her. She was a freelance journalist and very much into society gossip. I wasn't quite sure where she was going with her interrogation. Finally, she asked me the question that switched on the light in my head:

"You know what, Giselle? I would love to go to Monte Carlo with you. Let's make it a fun trip. Maybe we can meet Omar Sharif, and you can introduce me to him. What do you say? I am serious!"

It was much the same as with Jenny from CBC. The woman did not believe me.

"Sure," she laughed, "I would not admit it either."

The other customers sat there looking at me with mouths agape and curious eyes, none of them getting involved in the conversation. The four employees kept their eyes on their customer's toes. As I walked away, I thought about the implications of even more people spreading this ridiculous rumour. Because this second journalist brought it up, I was irritated. Me, of all people, having an affair with Omar Sharif? How silly. I decided it was time to check with my lawyer. He listened, grinning, and asked me,

"Giselle, is this true? Did you meet him in Las Vegas? Why not admit it, why should he not be a good friend to you?"

I was firm in denying it. He chuckled and gave me this advice:

"You know what? Let them talk. The next time someone confronts you with it, just smile and say 'no comment' and let it be. I must say, I get a kick out of it and, if nothing else, it's good for business."

He was right. The store was busier, and new people booked appointments hoping to catch a glimpse of me. For a short time, I was an odd celebrity.

When Doris invited me to her upcoming wedding, she added, "But please, don't bring Omar Sharif."

I looked at her, surprised she brought up the gossip. "You too? You don't believe it, do you? It's so ridiculous…"

Without looking up from the manicure she was doing, her answer was, "Oh yes, I believe it."

"Would it be all right if I bring the ABBA band?" I knew she loved this band.

"I would have to ask Dad about it. He's paying for the wedding." She was serious while I was joking. One of my wedding gifts was the newest ABBA record album.

After a few weeks, everything died down, and nobody ever mentioned it again. I tried for weeks on end with little comments, statements or questions to find the 'reliable source' within my employees. To my surprise, I succeeded a couple of years later. It was my expression, "Oh my…" that I had uttered, "oh my" when my secretary came and reminded me of a phone call she had put on hold ten minutes ago. "Oh my, oh my…" started it all. Weird, eh? Translate 'Oh my…' into 'Omar…' Since there was only one Omar known, the rumour was born and quickly escalated. Oh my - Omar was waiting on the telephone to speak to Giselle!

Moral of the story: Be aware of how you pronounce your words. This whole episode came back to me after I read the news

GISELLE ROEDER

of Omar Sharif's passing after a heart attack in Cairo on July 10th, 2015. RIP, my good old (unknown) friend…

FLIGHT INTO THE UNKNOWN

34: FIRST TRIP DOWN UNDER

Richard and I flew to Sydney for the Australian Health Food Convention in October. He was involved with an Aussi book import/export company. We visited all the tourist destinations. We took a city and a harbour tour, and we enjoyed a trip in a fast, so-called flying boat across the water to an island where we saw and learned all about Australia's wild dog, the Dingo. Unfortunately, I caught a debilitating flu. I was keen to visit the gorgeous Sydney Opera. After touring through the marvellous building, we saw the opera 'Toska,' not one of my favourites, but our only chance to get into the heart of things. I had an embarrassing cold and cough, suffered from a fever, felt miserable, and during intermission, Richard took me back to the hotel. He bought some cold medicine, which made me feel quite drowsy. The next day, we flew to New Zealand. He rented a small car in Auckland. After driving for about an hour, I was only half awake when I noticed a huge truck coming directly towards us. The driver was waving frantically. I quietly asked Richard,

"Shouldn't you be on the other side of the road?"
"Oh, my God, yes!!!"

There was only time enough to drive into the ditch on our right – or we would have been dead. Navigating the last traffic circle, Richard had unconsciously chosen the right instead of the left lane. Australians drive on the left side of the road. Boy, that was close! He thanked me for not screaming. If I hadn't woken up, he might have driven head-on into the truck. With lots of weight behind them, a truck cannot stop.

The truck did not slow down or stop. A couple of cars did and helped us to get our small vehicle out of the not too deep ditch. Both of us were now much more aware and paid close attention to driving on what was for us, the wrong side of the road. I felt responsible and kept an eye on Richard and his driving. After all, we were both jet-lagged. He begged me to keep him awake.

I liked New Zealand. It was so green, the hills dotted with white sheep. New Zealand has three million inhabitants, but 75 million sheep. October was spring-time, and masses of little lambs were born. They stayed close to their mothers or snoozed behind clusters of daffodils. These flowers bloomed everywhere, millions of them. We stopped several times to take photos of the sheep. But, whenever we got close to the fence along the highway, the sheep would turn and show us their backsides. To watch a sheep-shearing was quite an experience. After losing their coat, the sheep looked so naked. The shearers were quick and never hurt or cut the animals. It only took ten minutes, and the woolly fur was off.

We visited both islands. In Christchurch on the South Island, we experienced a downpour such as neither of us had ever seen. We went into the beautiful Christchurch Cathedral and waited for the rain to stop. It didn't, so we raced across the wet, glittering plaza into an ice cream parlour, later finding a hotel and continuing our tour across the island the next day. A massive ferry took us through the Wellington Canal back to the North Island. When entering the open sea, the waves were so high that they splashed the windows on the fifth floor! Unbelievable! Since the water is very salty, there were men busily washing the windows after our arrival.

On the return trip, we stopped for a few days in Fiji. Little green lizards crawled all over the wall in our hotel room and made funny noises. I was afraid. Richard found out that they eat mosquitoes, and they wouldn't fall onto our bed since it had a canopy. Good! The next night, we had a scary tropical storm, and everybody had to spend the night in the lobby. Another experience was a talk with one of the older employees, who had been a cannibal during his younger years. Creepy. He told us that human flesh tastes a bit between pork and chicken. At the beach, Richard

FLIGHT INTO THE UNKNOWN

rented a catamaran, and we enjoyed sailing over to an uninhabited island. On the way back, about a hundred meters from the beach, I decided to jump off and swim back. I almost drowned. Something was biting me on all the soft spots of my body, and it was impossible to get rid of whatever it was. Just as bad as the black mosquitoes on Lake Athapapuska. Exhausted from splashing and fighting, I arrived on the beach. The man, who had rented us the boat, explained,

"You shouldn't have jumped off the boat. Those are sandflies. They love white people. We are immune to them; they do not bite us."

I looked as if I had the measles. I never was a pool person, but from that day on, I preferred the large pool with a bar in the centre. We'd swim up to it, sit on an underwater stool and have a tropical drink. What a life!

The next stop on this incredible trip was Honolulu, Hawaii. Here, we parted. Richard continued his flight home to the USA. My Canadian plane was grounded, needing repairs. We had arrived at 8:30 AM, waited all day, received coupons for lunch, but were not allowed to leave. We were loaded at about 2:00 PM, taxied out to the runway and, after a few minutes, the plane turned around, and we were not happy to get off again. The airline gave us coupons for dinner, but we were not allowed to leave the airport. They finally put us into different hotels close to 11:00 PM. I had a kingsize bed all to myself.

Coming home to cold Winnipeg, I learned that I was a grandma. Doris had given birth to a little boy. The couple had bought a house on Beverly Street, north of Portage Avenue. Other news was that Louis now had a girlfriend. No, not 'that lady' I had predicted for him.

Christmas was sad for me this year. I had dinner with Marianne. Doris, her small family, and Eric spent the holidays with their dad. I had not heard anything from East Germany since I had been there in August. Since the death of my dad, I felt very alone in the world.

I had initially immigrated to Vancouver and started to think about moving back. I could handle my wholesale company from Vancouver. Most of my customers were in western Canada anyway. I didn't feel like taking my annual trip to Jamaica in

January and decided to fly to Hawaii. I had a tiny room with a narrow window (a former oversized broom closet) in the old Moana Hotel in Honolulu. I could hear the relaxing Hawaiian music in the evening and was always down at the beach for the sunset, waiting for the elusive 'green flash.' I never saw it.

I was back in Winnipeg for my fiftieth birthday at the end of January 1984. Marianne invited me to dinner, and she served me tasty home-made Eierlikör (a liqueur made from eggs and rum). Her cat was on my lap and purred a symphony. I got a bit tipsy and, unnoticed by Marianne, I let her lick my finger with some of the liqueur on it. She loved it and tried to put her paw into my glass to pull it closer.

It wasn't the future I had envisioned when I decided to follow my dream and emigrate to Canada, but I counted my blessings. I was NOT in the 'poorhouse' that Louis had promised me for my old age. He had handed me a lemon - so I would try to make lemonade.

In February, Richard invited me to come along to the US Health Convention in San Antonio, Texas. I had never been there and loved the idea. He asked me not to bring a coat. Strange. After a late arrival, we were planning to go for a walk along the small river and have dinner in one of the fancy little restaurants. I told him that I was too cold to go for a walk.

"No problem," he said, "here, put this on."

Flying towards me was a black and brown striped mink jacket.

San Antonio: I loved the city, and I started to not only like, but to love this man. Three days after the convention, we flew to Mexico for another week. An excursion to a famous snorkel resort could have been the end of me. He couldn't swim, but I wanted to snorkel. He rented gear for me and off I went, through a narrow gap in a rocky wall. I was sucked out into the wild sea before I knew it. I held a bag with bread pieces, and masses of fish surrounded me. I couldn't fight them or hold onto it and let it go. I realized that I needed to get back, but I couldn't handle the waves and the undertow. I tried to swim through that narrow gap, and every time I got close, a wave took me away. On my third try, I was afraid I would drown and tried to scream, but that didn't work underwater. Two ladies sat on the rocky wall; I stared at them and made a sign. They realized that I was in trouble. They jumped over

FLIGHT INTO THE UNKNOWN

to the small entrance. After several tries, they were able to catch my outstretched hand and pull me in. They helped me to a grassy area. Two tall, muscular men grabbed me by the legs and held me upside-down. I had swallowed a lot of water, was coughing and sputtering.

I wasn't the only one rescued. A well-known Mexican swimmer was unconscious when they pulled him out of the water. They were busy pumping his chest. When they put him on his side, water came gushing out of his mouth. I didn't feel grounded on terra firma and had to hold onto Richard. He was pale and couldn't believe that even an experienced swimmer had not been able to fight the waves. This experience changed my mind about oceans - or snorkelling in areas meant for more experienced people.

FLIGHT INTO THE UNKNOWN

35: THOUGHTS ABOUT MOVING

At Giselle's, the business was flourishing. Belinda had a good grip on it. She advertised daily on the radio. She changed a lot of things. Instead of my blue coverups for the customers, there were now thick, cozy white robes. She had lockers built into a closet for the customer's clothing and purses. I admired her greatly.

Doris had told me in March that she no longer wanted to have contact with me because her husband did not approve of it. Surprisingly, I received a letter from my mother. It brought me to tears. She complained about a lot of things, and towards the end of her letter, she wrote:

"I am 75 years old now, and nobody has room or time for me. I am not well. I wish you were here. I don't know what to do. Edith took charge of all my money. I have to ask if I need anything."

She must have cried when she wrote the letter as much of the writing was washed out. What could I do? I was in turmoil myself. I wrote to Edith and asked what we can do.

Our dad had a lawyer set up his will after one of my last visits. Due to East German restrictions, Christel and I had agreed that we forgo our inheritance in favour of Edith. Dad was unhappy about it and insisted that "things cannot go on as is. I believe there will be a change. And then, both of you will be glad to have a bit of money here." Germany reunited? That would never happen; how could Germany be reunited? He felt confident that it would. After mother, he named Edith as heir but had added her two teenage children. I did not know that. There was more money than either

Christel or I had expected. Edith was unhappy to share with her children. She argued, "what have the kids ever done for my parents?" Now, when mother needed her, Christel and I felt that she should look after her. I anxiously awaited her answer to my letter, but for the longest time, I heard nothing.

The Canadian Health Convention was in Vancouver this year. As always, I was booked as a speaker and had a booth at the exhibition. I hired Bella to help me. I had received several letters from her about problems in her personal life, but this is my memoir, not hers. I will never betray trust; my lips are sealed. To my disappointment, she had given up the small shop. She didn't pay the rent, so the shop owner kept the equipment. Easy come - easy go? My investment was lost. I had lost so much already; I felt helpless. We had some quiet mother-daughter talks, and I hoped she would be all right.

I stayed a few days longer in Vancouver. I was a guest on a popular radio show. I also visited my wholesale customers. My best one was a lady named Ilse Lander; she owned two stores. I saw her in her health food store in West Vancouver's Park Royal mall. I invited her out for coffee to privately discuss my intended move to Vancouver. She was excited and encouraged me.

Later that afternoon, I met with Nancy, a lady who worked for the Canadian Health Food Association. We met in the Danish Café on Robson Street. I told her of my plans, and she promised to help me in any way she could. After a quiet moment, she asked me,

"Have you ever had your cards read? Look towards the back of the café. The blond lady at the table covered in black is a fantastic tarot card reader. She is so spot-on. I know her; I'll introduce you when we finish our lunch."

I wasn't too keen on it, but Nancy convinced me. The lady's husband had founded a vitamin company; I had dealt with them for my health food store. As soon as the black table was empty, we went to see her. Miss X asked twenty dollars for a reading and invited me to sit down. I turned to my friend as she was about to leave:

"Don't go, Nancy, you must stay and write everything down. I am so nervous that I can't follow it and will miss or forget important things."

FLIGHT INTO THE UNKNOWN

It was exciting but also a disturbing experience. I couldn't believe how much the cards revealed about me and my circumstances. I had to choose a card after Miss X shuffled them and laid them out. Then another, and another. And so on. When she turned them around, there were pictures. She explained to me what they meant.

"You are presently very unhappy with your life. Your husband is deceiving you. You are anticipating a cross-country move. It will be to your advantage. You are in the process of buying a house with the help of a friend. Do not do that - it will tie you down. When you get home, you'll find that a young man has done something that will significantly upset you. You'll fight with him."

These were some of the most important messages the tarot cards sent me. How could all of this be in the cards? How did she know so much about me? We were strangers! I asked Nancy if she had told her about me before I came to the restaurant since she had already been there. She was adamant in denying it.

"No, Giselle, how could I! And I didn't know what you were going to tell me."

Right! She didn't. Nobody knew about my separation, about selling my business, about living apart from Louis. I had never told her that I had seen a condo in West Vancouver with a realtor in the morning. It was small, had two bedrooms and a large patio, but a fantastic view over the ocean towards Vancouver Island. I liked it but did not have enough money to pay for it. The realtor took me to his office, and I phoned Richard. I told him about it, and he offered to pay half. I wasn't comfortable with that and postponed my decision until after four o'clock. The realtor warned me that an old captain was also interested. I would have to make a quick decision. I didn't like to be pushed, took a chance, telling him to sell it to the old captain. If he bought it, then it wasn't mine in the first place. From his office, I went to meet Nancy. She didn't know about this. And who was the young man? I didn't have a young man in my life.

The realtor called me later at my hotel. I told him I decided not to buy it. He was disappointed, proclaiming he had kept it for me. He tried to talk me into it – but I did not change my mind. The tarot card with the picture of a woman with a rope tightly wound around her body was vivid in my mind. Nancy had recommended looking into apartment rentals in the Beach Avenue Towers. I was fortunate; one would be available at the beginning of June. It was a two-bedroom on the 21st floor. The rent was affordable. Now I had a time frame to organize my move.

I needed an office with a stockroom for my wholesale business. Fate was with me again. I visited our old friends, Hilda and George. She was looking after a small business building on Marine Drive in West Vancouver for their absent German friends. Downstairs was an antique shop, and on the second floor was a consulting business; two small offices and one quite large room without a window happened to be empty. It was perfect: one office for me, one for a secretary and the large one for a stockroom. My apartment was in Vancouver - it meant I would have to cross the Lionsgate Bridge every day. Since everything had fallen so nicely into place, I accepted that. We made a deal with a handshake for three years.

A few days after my return to Winnipeg, my son Eric turned up in my office. He told me he had dropped out of school. Was I horrified – six weeks before graduation? We had quite an argument, and he turned around and left. I was upset enough to phone Louis. He was bitter. He told me the school had called him, but he did not know where Eric was. He did not live with him any longer. Eric had told him, "I want to be free." Louis thought that he was with me and was surprised that he was not. The boy wasn't eighteen yet - I had not thought of him as a young man - but the tarot cards were right again. I was devastated. What could I do? We both hoped that Eric's common sense would kick in sooner or later, and he would come back home.

I started planning for my relocation. The moving company told me that my move would cost $6.00 per pound, plus loading time. I gave away quite a pile of books and advertised the Jacobean furniture set. A German man bought it. He paid less than I had spent at the auction, but he was happy, and I was glad to get rid of the heavy furniture. He called me several weeks later to thank me. He had it restored by a craftsman, and the estimated value for the insurance was now $48,000. Wow! Should I have taken it to Vancouver? The antique market there might be better than in Winnipeg. I congratulated him. I had no regrets. Too many memories - and $6.00 per pound? Moving it would have cost a mint.

I still had three regular office desks, two typewriter desks, a lot of shelving for the stockroom, loads of boxes with products and my stuff from the apartment. I sold most of the Gimli furniture, kept only some bookshelves and my bedroom set. Instead of a big moving company, I hired a U-Drive with a driver. My office files, my few valuables, my houseplants and my typewriter fit into my car. I vacated my apartment at the end of May, 1984.

Twenty years earlier, at the end of May, we had left Vancouver to move to Winnipeg when I was crying all the way to Lake Louise. Now, with my reverse move, I did not shed one tear. I estimated the drive would take me four or five days. I felt relaxed and drove at the posted speed limit. Once, looking into my rearview mirror, I saw an endless line of cars behind me. The highway was a one-lane with only occasional passing lanes. It was the stretch after Virden, between Manitoba and Saskatchewan.

All of a sudden, a police car came racing along, cutting into the traffic behind me, with their flashing lights and frightening siren warning me. I didn't know what I had done wrong. I kept driving until they were beside me and waved me over. I stopped on the shoulder.

"Lady, you are holding up the traffic. Get a move on! Or I'll issue a ticket!"

"Officer, I am driving within the posted maximum speed..."

"Sorry, lady, you'll have to drive faster to clear the lineup behind you."

"Okay, I can do that - but then I'll get a speeding ticket."

"No, you won't. You have to drive at the speed required by the traffic."

The cars, originally behind me, had now all driven past. I enjoyed driving faster, and I did not get a ticket, all the way to Vancouver. My car, a Mercedes 300TD, enjoyed the workout as well. Once the turbo kicked in, it was fun for both of us.

Oh, did I ever mention that the salesman's statement 'Buying a Mercedes is not an expense, it is an investment' had been right? It was in my case. I received every penny back - except for the tax - when I traded my 240D for this one. I practically drove my first Mercedes for 'free' for two years!.

FLIGHT INTO THE UNKNOWN

36 VANCOUVER - THE BEAUTIFUL

I arrived at my apartment on Beach Avenue in Vancouver a few hours before the U-Haul driver arrived with the truck. I had picked up my key at the rental office and had finished unloading my car. The driver was quick to help me bring up my personal belongings. The only thing we set up was my bed. We had to navigate the rush-hour traffic over the Lions Gate Bridge to West Vancouver to unload the business portion. The keys to my new office were in my purse; I had paid the rent ahead of time. It took us several hours. One desk into my office, two facing each other in the future secretary's office, all the product boxes into the stockroom.

I looked around at my new location and exhaled deeply. I drove back to Vancouver, didn't even change my t-shirt and jeans and went down to the beach. The sun was starting to set when I found an empty bench close to Second Beach. Two ladies nearby kept looking over to me and seemed to talk about me. Oh well, nobody knew me here, I didn't have to dress up or have my hair done when in public. That had been different in Winnipeg, because of my TV show, people would whisper when they saw me. I smiled, thinking of my lawyer. When I had told him that I planned to move to Vancouver, he had warned me:

"Giselle, are you sure? Think about it. In Winnipeg, you are a big fish in a small pond. In Vancouver, you'll be a tiny fish in a big pond. Is that really what you want?"

Yes, that was what I wanted. I stretched my arms out over the back of the bench. I looked up to the sky and sent a silent prayer of thanks. I enjoyed watching the glorious sunset over the ocean, adding a pink glow to the snow-capped Northshore mountains.

All the heartbreak was behind me. So I hoped. Is it true that everything happens for a reason? I had gone full circle: I was back where I started, to begin a new life in the city I had immigrated to, nearly twenty-one years ago, the town where I had wanted to be.

My Hanover boss used to tell me, "What doesn't kill you makes you stronger." I don't know if all I went through for the last few years did that - it might take me a while to build up my strength.

Once the sun was down, I walked over to those two ladies. Smiling at them, I asked,

"Why are you always looking over to me? What caught your interest from the moment I sat down?"

"Oh, Giselle, I was so happy to see you. I told my mother here how you changed my whole life. I attended one of your lectures at St. Michael's College in Toronto a few years ago. I had enrolled to study a different topic, but after listening to you, I changed it. I am now working at Blanche's Skincare Centre on Granville, and they slowly start to believe in what I bring to the table - your style of European skincare, based on health and nutrition."

I was stunned. So much for being a 'tiny fish' and not being known in Vancouver.

In deep thought, I walked along the beach, stopping at a small pizzeria on Denman Street, around the corner from my new home. Many little bistros with outside seating were along Denman. It was the road I would have to drive up to Georgia, make a left to go on through Stanley Park and across the Lions Gate Bridge on my daily commute to work.

That first night, all I wanted was a shower and then go to bed. I couldn't do it. Sleep wouldn't come due to brain overload. I started setting up the bedroom and unpacking the boxes marked clothing. I looked at the mess in the living room – but it was close to midnight, and I didn't want to annoy the people sleeping on the floor below me. Tomorrow was Saturday, with no alarm clock I could sleep in without feeling guilty.

Thinking of Scarlet O'Hara in 'Gone with the Wind,' I smiled to myself:

"I will deal with everything else tomorrow."

FLIGHT INTO THE UNKNOWN

EPILOGUE

After a good night's rest, tomorrow was now, and I faced a weekend with lots of work. But, I had no food in the fridge, so first things first. I was delighted by the many lovely shops and bistros, many with outdoor seating, in my new neighbourhood. Lots of trees and shrubs along the road, spring flowers in bloom, it was heaven! I gave in to the temptation to sit down, order a light breakfast and enjoy the morning sunshine; I couldn't help it, and why not? I had all the time in the world. I was not retired yet, tired maybe, but not retired, in charge of my own time. I found a Safeway shop further up the road, did my first necessary shopping and slowly walked back home.

Did the air ever taste and feel good! It was a beautiful Sunday morning close to the ocean, feasting my eyes on the blooming cherry trees and hundreds of daffodils. I had a hard time believing I wasn't dreaming. I almost felt delirious! Relaxed people were sitting everywhere; many were already at the beach playing frisbee or volleyball or leaning against the long thick tree trunks, pulled loose from log booms and brought to shore by wind and waves. It was a picture as if painted by Edouard Manet.

Reluctantly I started to work on my living room and kitchen. I unpacked every box, looked around, placed the bookshelves, filled them, unrolled the carpets, and even with just that, the room looked cozy. The paintings stood on spots along the walls; I realized I would need help to hang them up. I'd have to go and buy a couch, a table and a couple of chairs. Too bad, my small balcony did not face the ocean except for a limited view of it towards Stanley Park and the city. Illuminated at night, it was quite a change from Winnipeg. It was not large enough to sit out there; all the balconies at the higher stories were small, just big enough to step outside.

After taking the empty, flattened boxes to the underground garage to place them near the garbage bin, I got restless. The sun was past its zenith, and I needed to get out. During a pleasant afternoon walk along the beach and into Stanley Park, I watched the cricket players and discovered several tennis courts. Great, I would surely like to join the club and did so within a week. I played every morning from six to seven, different partners, different levels, sometimes even a double. I felt alive; life was good again.

It took me a week to set up and organize my business. The two offices were soon comfortable, but the storage room for the products was a complicated matter. But, when there's a will, there's a way. I felt I was well on my way to setting sail for life after 50.

~~~

ABOUT THE AUTHOR

Giselle Roeder is the author of several books, including "We Don't Talk About That." It is the first book of her trilogy-memoir. It describes her life in three Germanys: Her first ten years during the Nazi regime and surviving WWII, her teen years under communist rule in East Germany until her escape, and ten years in capitalist West Germany.

This book, "Flight Into The Unknown," tells the daring story of her marriage to an (unknown) Canadian pen-friend with a small daughter, followed by her immigration to Canada in 1963. It describes the ups and downs, trials and tribulations, living a newcomer's life, struggling with the language but becoming successful in business, a radio and television personality, an international speaker – but losing it all during the next twenty years.

The third book in this trilogy, "Set Sail for Life After 50" is a work in progress, with a publication date anticipated for September 2020.

Giselle has an inspiring personality, a memory like an elephant, enjoys speaking to high school students, Rotary/Probus and other clubs about the incredible life she lived.

www.ingramcontent.com/pod-product-compliance
Lightning Source LLC
Chambersburg PA
CBHW070543010526
44118CB00012B/1205